TOOLOOM GOLD RUSH - 1859

Tooloom Gold Rush - 1859

AND THE 'LADY BOWEN NUGGET'

Garry Gatfield

Jane Eberhardt

Grosvenor Creations

National Library Cataloguing-in-Publication entry

Author:	Gatfield, Garry J. G., 1951-
Title:	Tooloom Gold Rush – 1859 *and the 'Lady Bowen Nugget'*
Year of publication:	2024
Edition:	1st edition, revision 3.
Notes:	Includes Bibliography
ISBN:	978-0-6483184-1-5

Subjects:
1.Gold. 2.Goldfields. 3.Gold rush. 4.Gold nuggets. 5.Gold mines and mining. 6.Tooloom. 7.Lady Bowen Nugget. 8.Difflo. 9.Separation of Queensland. 10.Year 1859. 11.New South Wales. 12.Queensland. 13.Ipswich. 14.Warwick. 15.Grafton. 16.Casino. 17.Armidale. 18.Brisbane. 19.Pretty Gully 20.Clarence River District. 21.Drake. 22.Tenterfield. 23.Joe's Gully. 24.Australian History.

Grosvenor Creations
Brisbane, Queensland, Australia.

Cover Design by Ms Cathy Ball.
Editorial assistant – Ms Cassandra Gatfield.
Contributing Author and Editor – Jane Eberhardt

To contact the author about corrections, amendments or comments.
Email: goldpan@outlook.com

Dedication

To Grove, Milton and Carol
for all those golden days.

It was a pleasant life, and although disappointments were numerous,
yet the possibilities, if somewhat uncertain, were great.

Observation from an experienced gold miner - George Clark, describing the outlook of a typical digger during the gold rush era.

Preamble

When I first commenced gold prospecting at Tooloom in May 1980, I contacted the Mines Department in Sydney for any reports that they held on the Tooloom Goldfield. The following information is all that they could forward to me:

> *The Tooloom goldfield is situated some 35-40km north of Drake. Production of both alluvial and reef gold has taken place over a long period of time but the field as a whole is poorly documented. It is known that extensive alluvial gold workings existed along Tooloom Creek in the early 1870's and possibly prior to that date. Subsequently, quartz reefs were worked. However, no adequate description of the geology and mining history of the field is available. The only information available was that obtained in extracts from Annual Reports of the New South Wales Department of Mines (Gibbons, 1962). Total production from the Tooloom goldfield is not known.*

As you can no doubt appreciate from these comments, this part of north-eastern New South Wales really is a Forgotten Country' and, consequently, the title for Isabel Wilkinson's book on the Upper Clarence Goldfields, which was published in 1980, is most appropriate.

Later, when the Sydney mining company - Malachite Resources NL, started exploring the Tooloom Goldfield in 1997, they also claimed, with some justification, that it was a neglected and forgotten goldfield of New South Wales.

I hope the following makes some small contribution to the recorded history of Tooloom and the upper Clarence River goldfields.

Contents

Foreword

The development of modern Australia is intimately connected with the mining and extraction of wealth from the land. Indeed, Australia probably boasts the oldest mines in the world in the ochre mines of the McDonald Ranges, where many generations of Indigenous peoples have mined the coloured clays for ceremonial purposes.

Authors Garry Gatfield and Jane Eberhardt take us on an intriguing journey as they recount the comparatively recent history of how a small part of Australian wealth was won during the 1859-1862 gold rush days in the rolling bushlands of Tooloom in north-eastern NSW. By analysing contemporary newspaper reports and old letters, Garry provides us with a first-hand account of the trials and tribulations faced by the early prospectors and miners who rushed to Tooloom following the discovery of the 140oz 'Lady Bowen nugget' in 1859. At today's gold price of over $3,000 per troy oz, this would be worth about $450,000, which is enough to pay half the median price of a house in Brisbane! As Garry recounts, not only did the early miners have to face the challenges that were thrown up by Mother nature and by the lack of colonial infrastructure, they also had to risk their hard-won gold being stolen by bushrangers!

By 1862, most of the easy alluvial pickings from the Tooloom field had dried up and the miners then began to move on. Mining at Tooloom was, however, not done. In 1891, when cleaning out the rubble from the bottom of an abandoned shaft, John and Jack Payne discovered a 1.5 ft thick, gold-bearing vein. On the strength of this, the Rise & Shine Gold Mining Company of Tooloom was founded and went on to produce gold up until 1899. One can still visit the old Payne hotel (now a B&B) at Tooloom, which had been built in 1895 of local red cedar planks.

Jane Eberhardt then takes the reader on a fascinating journey into the geological genesis of the Tooloom gold field and this includes an analysis of the origin of the alluvial gold and of the subduction cycles of compression and extension, which had affected faulting and the subsequent emplacement here of orogenic gold deposits. One chapter also covers the tragic interactions between the squatters and the local Indigenous peoples. It especially highlights just how indispensable this Indigenous knowledge was in assisting the activities of the early European explorers in this east coast region of Australia.

The Australian gold rushes attracted a wave of young immigrants to this country and, by the early 1850's, the value of gold exports from Australia surpassed the export of wool; this enabled a higher standard of living for all Australians. Australia is a lucky country indeed! Just this year, the Australian Government announced an underlying cash budget surplus of some $22.1 billion. A closer analysis reveals that about one half of this was derived from the export of metallurgical and energy coals, with the other half coming from iron ore and other metal exports.

This book celebrates the pioneering characters who helped to discover, to develop and to extract our early gold resources. The development of modern Australia is intimately connected with the mining and extraction of wealth from the land.

Professor Peter Knights
Discipline Leader – Mining,
School of Mechanical and Mining Engineering,
The University of Queensland.

1

Introduction

Tooloom October 1860, by Conrad Wagner - Troopers conducting Licence inspection
Source: Courtesy of Mitchell Library, State Library, NSW, with permission.

The year 1859 had historical significance for New South Wales, but more particularly for Queensland, as that Colony first came into existence with the Proclamation of its official Separation from New South Wales in late 1859. The original Colony of New South Wales then lost a large portion of its northern frontier to Queensland with the signing of the Letters Patent by Queen Victoria on the 6th of June 1859; it was not until later in that year, however, when the first Governor of Queensland – Sir George Ferguson Bowen, arrived in Brisbane and read the Proclamation on the 10th of December 1859 that the fledging new Colony of Queensland finally came into official existence.

1859 was also the year in which gold was discovered at Tooloom. This book tells the history of the golden developments of the year 1859 as they relate to Tooloom in north-eastern New South Wales and of the effects of this discovery upon the young Colony of Queensland and upon the nearby towns of Brisbane, Grafton and Ipswich. These towns had provided the bulk of the diggers (miners) and services to the new goldfield of Tooloom from mid-1859 onwards.

This year (2024) is now the 165th year since the discovery of gold at Tooloom. The arrival of the magnificent Lady Bowen Nugget in Ipswich, on the same day as new Governor - Sir George Bowen's first official visit to that town on the 21st December 1859, occasioned great excitement in the new Colony of Queensland.

By 1859, the first decade of the gold rushes in Eastern Australia was drawing to a close but not without one last hurrah. This was an important year, not only in anticipation of forthcoming Separation, but also when the gold rush commenced at Tooloom and several large nuggets as well as many smaller ones were discovered. The most famous and largest of these was, of course, the 'Lady Bowen Nugget', which weighed 140oz 15dwt. This was found on the 8th of December 1859 at the mouth of Joe's Gully where it empties into Tooloom Creek. This author has attempted to document the big nuggets that were found within the rich gold claims of Joe's Gully and at various other golden gullies at Tooloom in 1859.

The Lady Bowen Nugget:

> *The nugget weighed 140 ounces in the gross and appeared to be nearly all virgin metal; quartz was observable only in the place where it was struck by the pick. In shape, it was a flat oval and nearly 2 inches thick in the thickest part. It was perfectly smooth on the surface as though it had been much subjected to the action of water. The lucky finders named their prize the 'Lady Bowen,' and, when it came down by the escort to Ipswich on Wednesday last, it was publicly exhibited to numbers for the price of one shilling.*
>
> (Source: *Moreton Bay Courier* 1846-1861 via Trove.)

Unfortunately, no photos were taken of this famous nugget at the time as far as I know but some reasonable descriptions were recorded.

Fortuitously, the nugget had arrived in Ipswich on the same day that the Governor and Lady Bowen conducted their first official visit. They were able to view the nugget first-hand at the residence of Colonel Gray. No doubt, Mr James Templeton - one of the finders and part owner of this large nugget, named it after her on the spot, as a gallant gesture to Lady Bowen.

Various newspapers in the Colonies of New South Wales and Queensland excitedly reported its discovery and arrival in Ipswich and shed further light on the 'Lady Bowen Nugget's' characteristics.

Lady Bowen, Contessa Diamantina di Roma, wife and consort of the first governor of Queensland - Sir George Ferguson Bowen
Source: Unknown, modified by Garry Gatfield, 2024

From *The Sydney Morning Herald*
26th of December 1859

Amongst numerous instances of successful mining in Joe's Creek [Gully], I was informed that McLean's party of four recently divided 500 hundred ounces of gold between them, the result of three months' labour.

A later stroke of fortune is that of Templeton and Co. who, when working last week in the same creek, procured the heaviest nugget that has been found on this Northern gold-fields weighing 140 ounces 15 dwts of pure gold. It was obtained about twenty yards above the spot where the eighty-ounce nugget was found some few weeks since.

This is the third time that this claim has been worked over by as many parties. The first merely ran a gutter up the centre when, believing it to be exhausted after obtaining a few ounces of gold, he sold his interest for £7; the second, a German, worked it a little wider and took out sixty ounces of gold in six weeks when, hearing of the rush to Emu Creek, he abandoned it for that locality and there did nothing; the third - the present holders, have worked it still wider and have procured more gold than either of the former parties - exclusive of the nugget previously mentioned.

This is the history of many of the most valuable claims in this district. I have noticed several on the Tableland and at McLeod's and Sandy Creeks, which were sold by the first holders for sums under £20 and which have since yielded gold to the value of several thousand pounds.

By early 1860, the famous nugget had finished it's sojourn in Brisbane and was then transported to Sydney for a brief public exhibition before ending up at its ultimate destination - the Sydney Mint.

The Sydney Morning Herald

21st of February 1860

The 'Lady Bowen Nugget' - along with the gold brought by the Telegraph Steamer to Sydney on her last trip from Brisbane, was a remarkably fine nugget that was found at Tooloom. Its weight is 140 ounces of solid gold; in shape it closely resembles a large yam; it is eight inches long, four and a-half inches broad at one end and tapers down to two and a-half at the narrowest part. It is two inches thick at the broad end. The value of this lucky find is, we believe, £500.

It has been called the 'Lady Bowen Nugget' in honour of the wife of the first Governor of Queensland. Through the kindness of the Bank of New South Wales, it will be on view at the well-known jewellery shop of Messrs Flavell Brothers and Co. in George Street, Sydney for a few days and it is well worth seeing.

As was all too common during the gold rush era, most of the gold nuggets were quickly sold and eventually ended up at the mint, where they were refined and minted into gold sovereigns.

The Moreton Bay Courier

Saturday evening, 15th December 1859 at Ipswich.

(From our own correspondent.)

Mr Ogilvy returned yesterday evening from the diggings, having left at 1 p.m. on Thursday last. About an hour before he left, a nugget of pure gold was found, which weighed 140 oz 15 dwts.

It was taken out of a claim at the foot of Joe's Gully that belonged to James Templeton of Brisbane and George Boyes; the latter was lately working on the Brisbane River Steamer.

Boyes has sent down 60 oz. of gold within the last three months. The nugget is in the charge of Sergeant Allan as I understand under promise that it shall be delivered in Brisbane.

Mr Ogilvy says that within the last fortnight there has been a very considerable quantity of gold found and that Tooloom assumes the appearance of a regular payable gold-field.

From the information gleaned from the above account of Ogilvy, we may surmise that the 'Lady Bowen Nugget' was found around noon on Thursday, 8th December 1859. We know with some certainty, the locality of the discovery; it was recovered from the alluvial drifts in the main bed of Tooloom Creek, where the junction of Joe's Gully meets the main creek.

We also know that it was in a sandy drift with some gravel and clay on the eastern side of Tooloom Creek opposite Joe's Gully. Part of this information was conveyed personally to me in June 1980, by the last remaining old prospector who was still living on the goldfield at that time. His name was Dave Smith and he had lived out his final days in a shack on the banks of Tooloom

Creek, downstream from the main bridge. He knew exactly where the 'Lady Bowen Nugget' had been found because he'd had personal contact with the earlier generations of diggers from the 1800's who also served out their time on the Tooloom goldfield. This information on the discovery and locality of such a large nugget had been generously passed on by those diggers because of the importance of such knowledge to future gold prospectors at Tooloom.

Dave Smith also told me that when the 'Lady Bowen Nugget' was found, it had been blackened on the side on which it had been lying in the creek. Gold miners in an earlier rush (1858) to Canoona in what became the new Colony of Queensland, had reportedly also experienced this phenomenon with some of the gold nuggets found there. Initially, many nuggets had been discarded for this reason until it had been belatedly realised that the 'black' was actually a coating of manganese (or sometimes, of iron oxide) over the gold. I have also found small nuggets with the same black coating on them on various goldfields.

Melchiorre et al., (2018) studied the occurrence of similarly blackened gold nuggets in placer deposits found at Rich Hill in Arizona USA; these researchers had concluded that such nuggets had come from a moist cavity in the bedrock or were from an area of high soil moisture from whence they had derived their blackened coating. This phenomenon of a black coating was subsequently identified as a complex assemblage of manganese, barium and iron oxide with elevated copper, all of which was most likely to have resulted from biological activity.

One correspondent– a local writer on the Clarence River Goldfields, has described how excited the Ipswich residents were when the nugget arrived and how it was then publicly exhibited for the cost of one shilling admittance. Whilst in Ipswich, the part-owner – James Templeton had declared that he had previously refused an earlier offer of six hundred pounds from a Grafton man. He said he preferred that it be sent to Sydney by way of Brisbane and, subsequently, offered to put it on display in Ipswich to raise money for the hospital. A prominent Ipswich citizen - Mr Warry, consented to take charge of the nugget and to host its public exhibition. This is an indication of just how hungry the public were for good news from the Tooloom goldfields.

Clarence River Gold, as found by the author and his cousin Milton
Source: Garry Gatfield, 2024

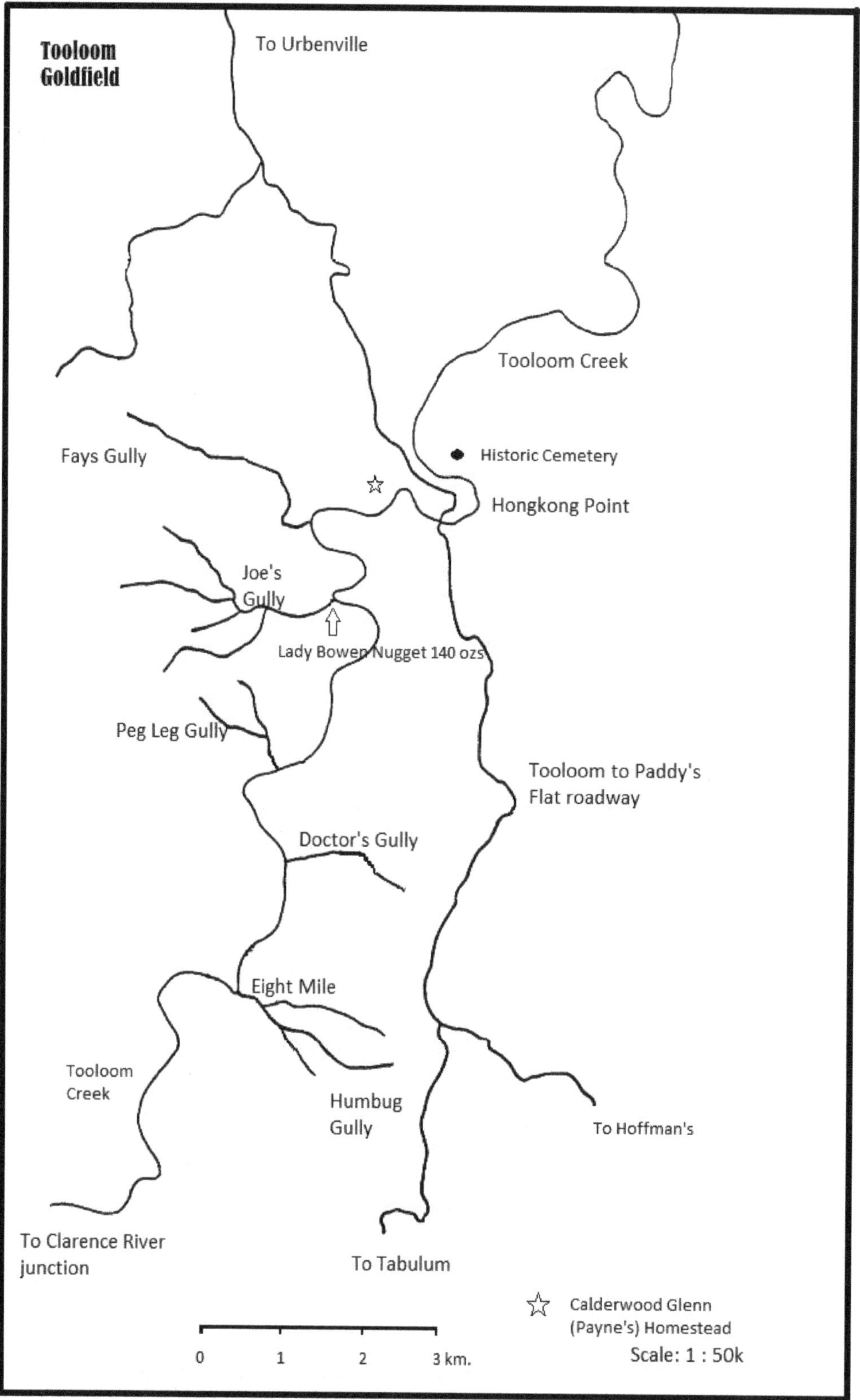

Figure 1. Tooloom Creek Goldfield Map
Source: Garry Gatfield, 2024

2

Gold Nuggets

A specimen of gold and quartz was reportedly found at Pretty Gully just south of Tooloom in late September 1861 by James McLaughlin; its gross weight was reported as 14lbs, which equates to 168oz. If a nugget of this size had been found at Pretty Gully, one would think that it would have been more widely known. The largest other nugget that I have seen recorded from Pretty Gully was 2ozs and my personal biggest nugget was only 1.5dwt. From this author's experience, Pretty Gully was not a nuggety field, so I am very sceptical about this claim.

The closest other large nugget localities to Tooloom were Warwick (65oz in 1895), Bingara (78, 60, 46.5ozs in 1852 and 42ozs recently), Kilkivan (100, 75ozs in 1867/8), and Gympie (975ozs in 1868). The Curtis Nugget from Gympie of 975ozs gross, with a net gold content of 906ozs when refined, was the largest nugget ever found in Queensland. Many other large nuggets and specimens were found at Gympie in addition to this nugget as mentioned above. The Sydney Mint paid £3,132/9/6 for the Curtis Nugget. Curtis was later sued by a former claim owner and lost thousands of pounds in Court and settlement costs.

I have listed the nuggets that can be validated from historical records for the Tooloom goldfield for the year 1859 only, and have compiled them in the following Table. There may have been other nuggets besides those listed that were discovered at Tooloom but some were not reported, as cautious miners preferred to keep the details strictly to themselves.

Newspaper reports of large nugget finds at Tooloom were regularly made and these reports were avidly read by the average citizen who, quite often, may have been considering whether to do a little mining for themselves. These reports fuelled the existing gold rushes at the time of the 1859 Tooloom gold rush. A typical report from the Clarence and Richmond Examiner follows:

THE TOOLOOM DIGGINGS.

To the Editor of the Clarence and Richmond Examiner.

Tubra Diggings, Tooloom Creek,
August 13, 1859.

SIR,—As an addenda to my last communication, I beg to inform you that I have just weighed three nuggets of gold—the respective weights of which are 5 ounces 18 dwts. 12 grs., 12 ounces 3 dwts., and 15 ounces 6 dwts. 12 grs.

The above speaks for itself; and notwithstanding the efforts of those whose interest it is to retard the progress of these goldfields, the Tubra Diggings will require no further comment from

Your obedient servant,
H. M.

I have opened this letter to inform you that another nugget has been found here, only weighing 40 ounces—very unsatisfactory!

A reliable nugget report from Tooloom
Source: Clarence and Richmond Examiner via Trove

The correspondent who signed himself as H. M. seems to have been a reputable storekeeper or gold buyer or both and he was also someone who could weigh a large nugget down to a one grain accuracy; for this, his gold scales had to be fairly precise. This is thus a good example of a typical report that I have relied upon.

Another example of a newspaper report, which gives a detailed account of the 15.82oz nugget found by *Black Dan* in Joe's Gully in August 1859, follows:

> *The memorandum of the particulars for the purchase of the 15oz nugget, which was on view in Mr Given's window (Ipswich), as No.11,062. Its weight before melting was 15.82oz, its weight after melting was 12.06oz. An assay report of fineness was 91.3%. It was also valued at £3 17s 10½d minus the Mint charge and the gold duty with a net value of £44 16s. 8d.*

Note: these details were extracted from the official memorandum from the Sydney Mint.

Table 1. Nuggets that were found at Tooloom during 1859:

Name of nugget	Weight of nugget	Date	Finder	Locality
The Lady Bowen Nugget	140oz 15dwt	8 Dec 1859	James Templeton and George Boyes	At the junction of Joe's Gully and Tooloom Creek
	80oz 17dwt 12gr	Early Nov 1859		
The Difflo Nugget	80oz 16dwt 6gr	27 Sep 1859	Charles Difflo	20 yards below the 'Lady Bowen Nugget'
	41oz	Aug 1859		
	15.82oz	Aug 1859	Black Dan	Joe's Gully (possibly)
	15oz 6dwt 12gr	Aug 1859		
	14oz	Aug/Sept 1859	Black Dan	Joe's Gully (possibly)
	12oz 3dwt	Aug 1859		
	10oz	Jun/July 1859		
	9oz	Sep 1859		
	7.5oz	Jul/Aug 1859		
	5oz 18dwt 12gr	Aug 1859		
	5.5oz	1859		
	4oz 10dwt	Jun 1859		
	4oz 2 dwt	Jul/Aug 1859		
	3oz 15dwt	Jun 1859	Big Joe	Joe's Gully – Probably, 4 ft deep.
	3.5oz	July/Aug 1859	Mr Broadhurst	4ft deep
	3oz 4dwt	July 1859		

Source: Garry Gatfield, 2024

Table 2. The Tooloom gold rush timeline:

Date	The Tooloom gold rush timeline
1859-60 only:	
Feb/Mar	Three different prospecting parties departed the Timbarra/Fairfield district to prospect for gold further north and east of Drake.
April – Easter	The discovery of gold at Tooloom by Perkins and party.
May 14 May late	Perkins announced the discovery of gold at Tooloom and returned to Tooloom after resupplying. The Tooloom gold rush slowly develops
June 6	The 'Letters Patent for Separation' were signed by Queen Victoria. Nuggets up to 10oz had started to be found at Tooloom. A new minor rush commenced to Emu Creek.
July	The Tooloom rush continued to develop - 500 diggers were then on the field.
Aug.	The first large nugget of 41oz nugget was discovered at Tooloom. The first private Ipswich gold escort arrived in Tooloom.
Sept. Sept. 27	Charles Difflo discovered his 80oz nugget in Joe's gully at Tooloom. Perkins letter claiming discovery of gold at Tooloom is published.
Oct.	Tooloom was officially gazetted as a goldfield. The Pretty Gully rush commenced.
Early Nov. Nov. 26	A second large nugget of 80oz was discovered. The 'Special Correspondent' commenced his journey to Tooloom from Brisbane.

Dec. 8	The 140oz 'Lady Bowen Nugget' was found by James Templeton and George Boyes at junction of Joe's gully and Tooloom Creek.
Dec. 10	Queensland's official Separation from NSW was announced.
Late Dec.	The 'Special Correspondent' arrived back in Ipswich.
Dec. 21.	The 140oz nugget arrived in Ipswich, was viewed by Governor and Lady Bowen and promptly named the 'Lady Bowen Nugget'.
Dec. 24	A Brisbane reporter gave a detailed description of the 'Lady Bowen Nugget' in the *Moreton Bay Courier.*
Late 1859	The official gold escort included Tooloom in its service to the Sydney Mint via Grafton.
1860:	
Feb. 21	The 'Lady Bowen Nugget' was displayed after its arrival in Sydney.
Mid May	The 'Difflo Nugget' Case was heard in the Supreme Court in Brisbane.

Source: Garry Gatfield, 2024

The price of gold in 1859:

The international price of gold remained fixed for nearly 200 years from 1717 until W.W.I. The price had been set at £4¼ by Sir Isaac Newton as Master of the Royal Mint, (Newton actually set the price at £4 4s 11½, which was out by 1 halfpenny). This fixed price of £4 4s 11½d was for 1 troy ounce of 24kt gold (99.5% fine or better depending on the particular refinery). As found by the Tooloom diggers, their alluvial gold was usually around 88-93% purity and most of it ended up at the Sydney Mint.

A digger on the goldfield would always get less than the full official gold price. The storekeeper had a profit margin to satisfy and the cost of transport, whether by official armed government escort or by private escort, also cost the digger a further percentage; then there was the shipping cost to Sydney to deliver it to the Mint and this was followed by additional charges for refining and for the smelting of the gold. All these additional costs amounted to a fair margin and, consequently, the price paid for Tooloom gold at £3 7s or £3 8s per troy ounce was approximately 80% of the official price.

This was a typical arrangement on all goldfields, throughout the gold rush era in Australia. The only cost factors that usually varied were the purity of the local gold and the transport costs, which depended on the distance of the diggings from Sydney, Melbourne or Perth. If the digger wanted to avail himself of a slightly higher price in the city, he usually had to give up work and travel considerable distances, all with the added security risks that were posed by the bushrangers. In the end, it was usually not worth the effort, so the diggers just accepted the price that was paid on the field; this price was usually reasonable, because of the number of competing buyers.

In the 20th century, the price of gold remained heavily regulated and even the private ownership of gold was declared illegal during the Depression era in 1933. Nearly 40 years later in 1971, U.S. President Nixon was finally forced to act; he removed the gold backing from the U.S. Dollar, thus allowing the price of gold to float. President Nixon also removed the restrictions on private ownership of gold and Australia followed his lead shortly afterwards. The President was forced to act because of the woeful economic situation that the U.S. faced, particularly in its' worsening balance of trade deficit and by the mounting national debt from the Vietnam War.

Gold has had a remarkable ride since that important decision in 1971 – but that is another story!

Small nuggets from the Clarence River goldfields
Source: Garry Gatfield, 2024

3

Gold discoveries in Eastern Australia

Ipswich and Moreton Bay probably supplied the bulk of the diggers who rushed to the Tooloom goldfield in 1859 because these towns, which had large numbers of itinerant but willing man-power and were able to capitalise on the discovery, were the closest major settlements to the new diggings. The remaining overland-arriving diggers came from nearby localities such as from the Timbarra goldfields; more also followed from Grafton, Tenterfield and Uralla and many sea-going participants also arrived via coastal shipping through Grafton and Moreton Bay. Many citizens from Ipswich and Brisbane (the Moreton Bay Settlement) optimistically referred to the Tooloom Goldfield as 'our goldfield' in those heady early days of 1859.

Most readers would probably be aware that the Australian gold rushes had officially commenced in 1851 with the announcement of the discovery of gold at Summer Hill and Lewis Ponds Creek near Bathurst in New South Wales. This site became known as Ophir after King Solomon's famous gold mine and the first gold 'rush' then commenced in April 1851. This gold discovery was publicised by Edward Hammond Hargraves but the gold was actually found by William Tom and John Lister whilst Hargraves was absent in Sydney. Hargraves received all the recognition and a government reward but this travesty remains on our history books. We are not here, however, to debate this historic oversight but merely to set the scene for the relevant events leading up to the year 1859.

The first major gold discoveries in New South Wales had initially been centred around Bathurst with rushes then spreading from Ophir to Sofala, to the Turon, Hill End, and to Louisa Creek, all in central New South Wales. These were followed shortly thereafter by rushes to the Shoalhaven, Araluen, Braidwood, and to the Major's Creek district to the south of Sydney.

The NSW goldfields had also gradually spread northward from Bathurst to Hanging Rock, to Nundle and to the Peel by late 1851 to early 1852. These gold finds were then soon followed by Bingara in May 1852, whilst gold in the other Rocky River at Uralla to the south of Armidale was first discovered in 1852 but it wasn't until 1854 before the first major rush developed there. Then came the Oban in mid 1856 and this was followed by the discovery of gold at McLeod's Creek and Timbarra in 1857, then at Boonoo Boonoo in early 1858 (where Banjo Paterson met his future wife).

Numerous goldfields had also been opened-up in Victoria by late 1851. Over the decade of the 1850s, large numbers of diggers had fanned out in search of gold. Many diggers were always ready to head off to the latest rumoured gold rush. Some were paroled convicts but new migrants in search of golden opportunities were in the majority within the year.

In Victoria, the major gold rushes were more concentrated around the central part of that colony. Victoria had achieved its own separation from New South Wales in 1851 with the concurrent discovery of major alluvial goldfields. Clunes was first in mid 1851 and, soon after, came Ballarat, Castlemaine and Bendigo.

Prior to the discovery of gold at Tooloom, probably about 1,000 gold-diggers were already chasing the elusive metal at various fields centred on the small settlement of Fairfield, which is now known as Drake. They were gainfully employed on the Timbarra River, at McLeod's Creek and on the Timbarra Tableland, which stretched from Sandy Creek to Poverty Point and Surface Hill and to the various small streams, which drain the Timbarra Tableland into the Timbarra River. This was just in time for our story to begin at Tooloom in 1859.

The first major gold rush had occurred in the year before - 1858, at Canoona to the north of Rockhampton in Queensland. This field was small and had been overwhelmed by at least 20,000 southern diggers. This later led to the arrival in Tooloom of a large band of disgruntled diggers who had been looking for new opportunities in the soon-to-be separate Colony of Queensland; those that had not already been repatriated south to Sydney or Melbourne by late 1859 then became participants in the Tooloom gold rush.

For the gold diggers travelling towards the Clarence River in mid 1859, the stories that they were hearing about the riches of the Timbarra and McLeod's Creek would have provided great encouragement for them to also push onwards and to seek good claims at the new gold strike at Tooloom.

The discovery of gold at Tooloom in early 1859:

It was a regular custom of the diggers on proven goldfields like the Timbarra and McLeod's Creek to go prospecting in their vicinity. We know that at least three prospecting parties had left the Fairfield (Drake) township or Timbarra fields to prospect for gold further to the north and northeast of the Drake district in early 1859. At least one party ventured too far to the east and only discovered coal; they returned disheartened! The prospecting party led by Perkins obviously had more success as the following letters show.

Fearing an exodus of their own much-needed workers, the leading citizens of Moreton Bay and Ipswich had also recently offered a sizeable reward for the discovery of a payable goldfield nearby in the hope that they might all profit from it; this reward from Brisbane was, however, never paid out to the discoverers of the Tooloom goldfield!

The discovery of the Tooloom goldfield in the first half of 1859 was claimed by Perkins and his party. Many writers have since attributed this discovery to Willian 'Billy' May in 1857 who was not named anywhere in the literature of that period (1857-59). I surmise, however, that he may have been an unnamed member of the Perkin's Party. Nowhere is there any record of May claiming the title of discoverer of the Tooloom goldfield for himself. Big Joe of Joe's Gully fame also attempted to claim the honour of discovery, as did another party.

A meeting of miners and the Timbarra Sub-Gold Commissioner subsequently denied both the latter claims and awarded the title of discoverer of the Tooloom goldfield to the former Perkins and his party.

The following letters recorded the claim of the discovery:

The Clarence and Richmond Examiner, 28th of June 1859.

A correspondent of the *Clarence and Richmond Examiner* wrote:

Table Land, McLeod's Creek:

Three hundred men left here yesterday for the new Tooloom Diggings, which by old experienced diggers are pronounced likely to become rich and flourishing diggings; the gold is large and coarse and is met with in crevices, in gullies, and in the beds of creeks.

The diggings at McLeod's Creek are good rich diggings and are, without doubt, lasting. I am now at the centre of the Tableland and, taking a circuit of twenty miles, gold is found in every gully and creek and particularly in the creeks that are tributaries of the Rocky, of which there are a great number. Indeed, it extends right away to Glen Innes and will no doubt prove a most valuable and extensive goldfield. Nothing but the bed of gullies have yet been worked but there are good rich payable veins that only requiring sinking.

The following letters by Coley and Perkins and Co were published in the Moreton Bay Courier in late September 1859; this was well after the event. They were the first to lay claim to the honour and promised reward for a discovery of gold close to Brisbane in April 1859; this letter below had been forwarded to the Moreton Bay Courier by Brisbane businessman – Capt. Richard J Coley on the 26th of September 1859.

Letters to the Editor of the Moreton Bay Courier
North Brisbane, 26th of September 1859.

Sir, I beg to hand you a second letter for publication, received by me from James Perkins and Co. containing further particulars for the information of the citizens of Brisbane in which they seek to prove themselves the finders of the Tooloom gold field and, to urge upon the Brisbane people, their claim to the (promised) reward as the finders of those diggings.

Yours truly, Richard J. Coley.

Tubra Diggings, Tooloom Creek,
20th of September 1859.

Sir, - Yours of the 12th instant duly came to hand and we are very much obliged to you for the information and advice that you have given us. We should have been more explicit but we thought you might probably have seen that the public prints everything connected with the diggings. We are happy to give you all the information that you require. (Note: 'Tubra' is the original indigenous name for this locality).

We discovered these diggings in April last (1859). We found the first payable gold here on what we call a 'bar' in the bed of Tooloom Creek and we prospected the ground and found it payable (as in being able to make a living from it). We marked off our ground, left some of our tools and a tent and started back to the Fairfield (Drake) diggings, where we had left one of our mates, and some tools etc. We took from here, five dwt, of gold as a sample that we got in the claim within which we are now working.

Mrs Smith of the Clarence Inn now has this gold in her possession; we left it with her to be shown to anyone whom she thought proper. Several diggers saw it; there was a rush here and some of them have succeeded in finding good claims. Shortly afterwards, there was a public meeting of the diggers and I, on behalf of myself and my partners, applied for our extra claims as the discoverers of this gold field. The diggers admitted our claim and awarded us the extra claims that we were entitled to. Another party led by Big Joe also applied for it but his claim was rejected by the diggers, for we had found payable gold here and had commenced work a month before he arrived on the diggings. Subsequently, the Commissioner came here and confirmed our right to the prospector's claims and refused Big Joe's; we can bring forward evidence to prove that we are the bona fide discoverers of the Tooloom diggings.

The reason we did not apply for the reward before was that we wanted the diggings to be developed and to prove payable. The diggings have done so, which is proved by the number of men who are working here and doing well. You will see by the Ipswich papers that there is a subscription already opened (for us) by the Ipswich people.

The first gold that we sent from here was 12ozs 10dwts. It realized £3 7s 11d per ounce at the Mint. There has since been a considerable number of nuggets found here; a man found one last week weighing 9oz and I held it in my hand. He got 20 oz in three days and he had been on the diggings only a fortnight. We arrived here when we came for good on the 14th of May.

We shall be most happy to give you any information that you may require. We are very grateful for your kindness and believe us to remain, Sir.

Your obedient servants

James Perkins and Co.

To Capt. Coley.

Capt. Richard J Coley was a prominent Brisbane businessman and was a member of the Moreton Bay Courier's Committee, which was formed in 1851 to push for Separation; he was also on the Gold Discovery Reward Committee. Capt. Coley was the first appointment to the largely ceremonial position of Sergeant-at-Arms of the Queensland Parliament and he was most probably one of the founders of the Brisbane Chamber of Commerce and was an early Chairman.

Finally, a reward for Perkins and party:

The Moreton Bay Courier (Brisbane, Qld.)

Thursday 16th of August 1860.

A liberal reward!

> *Sir, Permit us through the medium of your journal to return our grateful acknowledgements to the liberal people of Ipswich for the very munificent sum of nine pounds awarded to us for the discovery of the Tooloom gold-fields.*

Perkins' party.

As mentioned earlier, Perkins and his party never received the promised reward offered by the leading citizens of Brisbane, but at least they enjoyed a small consolation prize from Ipswich! When James Nash discovered gold at Gympie in October 1867, unlike Perkins, he was handsomely rewarded, but the goldfield was within Queensland, whereas Tooloom ended up in NSW.

The author fossicking for gold Tooloom 1980
Source: Garry Gatfield, 2024

4

Governance on the goldfields of NSW

After 1823, there had been numerous reports of small gold discoveries in both New South Wales and, in what was to become, Victoria by 1851. These reports were however, all suppressed by the Colonial Governor - Sir Charles Fitzroy and by Colonial Secretary Edward Deas Thompson. Together they feared the likely civil unrest and chaos that must inevitably be associated with such news in what was, essentially, still a penal colony. The news promulgated by Edward Hammond Hargreaves of the discovery of gold at Ophir in 1851 was, however, more difficult to suppress. The Californian gold rushes had commenced in 1848 and news from those diggings had received widespread attention throughout the world. Many would-be diggers from New South Wales had already departed for those goldfields on the accessible west coast of the United States. (It was easier to sail from Sydney to San Francisco, than for a New Yorker to sail from the East Coast of the USA, to California).

The 'Letters Patent' for the Separation of Queensland from the Colony of New South Wales:

These were personally issued by Queen Victoria to Sir George Ferguson Bowen on the Isle of Wright in the United Kingdom on the 6th June 1859.

The *Moreton Bay Courier, Brisbane.*

10th of December 1859.

Letters Patent in reference to the Separation of Moreton Bay.

Ordered by the Legislative Assembly to be printed on the 29th of November 1859.

W. Denison, Governor-General of New South Wales.

> *The Governor-General lays before the Legislative Assembly, a copy of the Letters Patent erecting Moreton Bay into a Colony under the name of Queensland, and for appointing Sir George Ferguson Bowen, K.C.M.G., to be Captain-General and Governor-in-Chief of the same. Also, a copy of the Order in Council empowering the Governor of Queensland to make laws and to provide for the administration of justice in the said Colony (is included).*

Under the provisions of this latter document, certain duties had also been imposed upon the Governor-General of New South Wales.

> *In accordance with the directions contained in a despatch from the Secretary of State, a copy of which was laid before the Legislative Assembly on 11th October last, no Separation is to take place until these Letters Patent have been published both in New South Wales and in Queensland. The Governor-General has, therefore, given directions for the publication of these Letters Patent and for notifying the fact that from and after the 1st of December next ensuing, the Legislative Authority of the Governor and Legislature of New South Wales and the power of such Governor over the territories comprised in the said Colony of Queensland and over the Revenues thereof, will cease.*

The *Letters Patent* as presented above in Sydney were the official documents presented to Sir George Ferguson Bowen by Queen Victoria, which effectively then led to the creation of the new Colony of Queensland in December 1859. *Letters Patent* are a form of open or public proclamation and a vestigial exercise of extra-parliamentary power by a Monarch. Prior to the establishment of the Parliament, a Monarch ruled absolutely by the issuing of their personal written orders, open or closed, with their seal.

Determining the New South Wales northern border from Queensland after Separation in December 1859:

Many people in the Moreton Bay District in mid-1859 regarded the Tooloom Goldfield as part of Queensland but was it? The *Letters Patent* issued to Sir George Ferguson Bowen on the 6th of June 1859 pursuant to Section 7 of the New South Wales Constitution Act of 1855 commissioned him as the first governor of the new Colony of Queensland but the actual land border between the two colonies had still to be defined. The Colony of New South Wales had a surprise in store for both Grafton and Ipswich and, on 1st December 1859 and proclaimed and described its north-eastern border as:

> *We have, and of all other powers and authorities in us that behalf vested separated from Our Colony of New South Wales and erected into a separate colony so much of the said Colony of New South Wales as lies northward of a line commencing on the sea coast at Point Danger, in latitude about twenty-eight degrees eight minutes south and, following the range thence, which divides the waters of the Tweed, Richmond and Clarence Rivers from those of the Logan and Brisbane Rivers, westerly to the dividing range...*

This description was a surprise, but it should not have been. In 1839, the British Government had been looking to form a new penal colony in New South Wales for transportation and for secondary punishment; the then Secretary of State for the Colonies – Lord John Russell, favoured Moreton Bay for a northern boundary from New South Wales. In 1841, his successor – Lord Stanley, was also in favour of this site and envisaged sending reformed and discharged convicts to Moreton Bay where they would become self-supporting farmers so that they would not be a drain on the Colonial Government for their financial support. The Moreton Bay District had then been established under the 1839 Squatting Act with a definition based on natural features for the first time, as reported in the New South Wales Government Gazette of 10 May 1842 as follows:

> *Bounded on the south by the ranges, which separate the sources of the rivers Brisbane and Logan from those of the Clarence and Hunter ...*

In 1842, the British Government had also added a proviso into their Act of Partition for the New South Wales Colonial Government that stated:

> *Provided always that no part of the territories lying southward of 26°S be detached from the said colony (5 & 6 Vic.c.76, see section 4).*

In October 1846, a new site for another northern colony was proposed and was just to be called the North Colony; Colonel Barney was appointed the Lieutenant Governor and Port Curtis was chosen as the new administrative centre. The North Australia Proclamation was issued on the 30th of January 1849, which assigned all lands lying to the north of 26°S to this new colony and Deputy Surveyor General to the Colonial Secretary - Mr S Perry, wrote that he had directed Mr Warner in the Northern District to trace the watershed of the Brisbane and Boyne Rivers and:

> *Having ascertained the principal sources of the latter river, to trace it down to the 26th parallel of latitude, then to run that latitude to the coast.*

As a point of interest, settlers did actually arrive in Port Curtis but, after a change in the government in England in 1846, the new Secretary of State for the Colonies – Earl Grey, issued orders to abandon the newly established colony.

One of the most prominent political activists in New South Wales – the Reverend John Dunmore Lang, was particularly disappointed by this decision. He had been arguing for the establishment of a new colony north of 30°S Latitude, which he envisioned would be populated by protestant farmers. Neither the new Governor (and Governor-General) of New South Wales – Sir William Denison, nor the local colonial squattocracy liked Lang's ideas at all and, in 1855, they joined forces against him. The latter considered that latitude 30°S would be a big problem for the export of their wool through the inland port of Grafton and might also put pressure on their existing pastoral leases for the release of more land. Lang had previously successfully lobbied the Crown in England, when he had insisted that any new colony could be created northward of the 30°S latitude provided that a petition be received from the residents of such area. The following proviso was then quickly inserted by Governor Denison's supporters in turn; these hoped that there would not be a northern boundary fixed at the thirtieth parallel:

> *Provided that always: 'That nothing herein contained shall be deemed to prevent her Majesty from altering the bounds of the Colony of New South Wales on the north as to how Her Majesty shall deem fit.'*

The description of the northern border in June 1859 with it placed at about 28°S was quite unexpected. Perhaps it was some sort of compromise by Her Majesty between Governor Denison and his supporters and those of Reverend Lang's.

> *Now know you, that we have, in pursuance of the powers vested in us by the said Bill and Act and of all other powers and authorities in us that behalf vested separated from Our Colony of New*

South Wales and erected into a separate colony so much of the said Colony of New South Wales as lies northward of a line commencing on the sea coast at Point Danger, in latitude about twenty-eight degrees eight minutes south and following the range thence, which divides the waters of the Tweed, Richmond and Clarence Rivers from those of the Logan and Brisbane Rivers, westerly to the dividing range ... and erect the said Territory so described into a separate Colony to be called the Colony of Queensland.

The Australian Colonies Act of 1861 (often called the Queensland Government Act) in Sections 2, 5 and 6 had thus made provision for rectifying any mistakes by either contiguous colony, which could, as long as royal assent had not yet been given and with the advice of their executive councils, alter the colony boundary.

Whereas the boundaries of certain of Her Majesty's Colonies on the Continent of Australia may be found to have been imperfectly or inconveniently defined and it may be expedient from time to time, to determine or alter such boundaries: Be it, therefore, further enacted as follows ...

Letters Patent on the 13th March 1862 were made under this Australian Colonies Act 1861 (UK) pursuant to section 2, which stated that:

Queen Victoria annexes to the Colony of Queensland 'so much of Our Colony of New South Wales as lies to the northward of the 26th parallel of south latitude, and between the 141st and the 138th meridians of east longitude, together with all and every (part) of the adjacent islands, their 'members and appurtenances in the Gulf of Carpentaria.'

The precedence for the use of natural features for defining the border had long been in use in the Colony of New South Wales and continued whilst the 26th Parallel was, thus, also then accepted and so the Tooloom goldfields were now lost to Queensland, having been caught in the political crossfire between the Colonial Government in Sydney and the Reverend J D Lang and his supporters.

The official border had been determined by agreement of both colonies in 1859 and was then surveyed by Surveyor Rowland from New South Wales in tandem with Surveyor Roberts from Queensland. Roberts had endeavoured to keep as many straight-line segments in his traverse as he could (he was acting on implicit instructions from Queensland) and often deviated from the crest of the dividing watersheds of the above streams. Nevertheless, it was Robert's survey that was most often accepted, but the critical positions of the border line did not always coincide for the two surveyors.

The relevant *Letters Patent* were published in Brisbane by Government Notice dated the 21st of June 1859. The New South Wales Government Gazette had proclaimed the establishment of the new Colony of Queensland and described the boundaries of this new Colony on the 1st of December 1859. The Queensland Government Gazette followed on the 10th of December 1859.

A Proclamation declares a new goldfield in the New South Wales Government Gazette:

On the 14th of October 1859, Tooloom was officially gazetted as a goldfield:

The gold-field on Crown Lands at and in the vicinity of Tooloom Creek, and its tributaries from its confluence with the Clarence River to its tributaries are declared to be a Gold-Field, within the meaning of and for the purpose of the Act of Council, 20th Victoria, No. 29.

Typical diggers camp as captured by Daintree
Source: Daintree, State Library of Queensland, out of copyright

5

The Gold Commissioner System

John Richard Harvey - the first Commissioner for Crown Lands for the goldfields, had been the Police Magistrate for Parramatta and, in May 1851, he was appointed Gold Commissioner by Governor Fitzroy and Colonial Secretary Deas Thompson; Harvey was then sent off as soon as they could organise it to Ophir to begin issuing gold-mining licences on Crown Lands. Harvey was a wise choice by the colonial administration. The Commissioner System then operated successfully in New South Wales until 1874 under his careful and judicious leadership (Hamilton, 2014) but a similar system in Victoria was replaced by 1855 after the Eureka Stockade event, which severely discredited the Commissioners on the Victorian goldfields.

The February 1853 Act for regulating the management of the goldfields of New South Wales and *'for raising a Revenue therefrom and for the Preservation of Order thereon'* then led to the further appointment of thirteen Commissioners who were each appointed for their respective Crown Lands District; these were also granted wide powers over each gold digger therein. These powers included being able to determine the extent and provision of each person's claim and to mark their claim. The Commissioner could also, without a warrant, arrest and detain any unlicensed person found mining or digging for gold on the proclaimed goldfield. Besides being entitled to raise revenue from the sale of licences, the Commissioner was also given the power of arbitration to settle any encroachment disputes and was also responsible for setting up the gold escort systems for safely transporting the individual miner's gold to the Sydney Mint. These powers were initially applied only to public lands but they were subsequently extended to cover gold-mining areas on private land with the said owner's permission.

These thirteen Commissioners for the New South Wales goldfields were left under no illusions as to how far the Governor's and the Colonial Secretary's management priorities extended for them beyond mere revenue raising, when they were all addressed by Colonial Secretary Deas Thompson before their departure to their new positions.

Colonial Secretary Thompson's instruction to NSW Gold Commissioners, 23rd of May 1851:

> *Though your chief business will be to protect the interests of the Crown in matters of revenue, it will be an essential part of your duty to preserve the peace, to put down outrage and violence, and to protect the community generally.*

A Commissioner was appointed to the Northern Gold district, which included New England and he was located at Nundle. He was assisted there by the subsequent appointment of Sub-Commissioners who were located at Timbarra, Rocky River and Babeewarilla. The Commissioner or Sub-Commissioner was essentially both an administrator and an adjudicator of the many small disputes, which so often arose on the early goldfields in New South Wales. These usually required a quick resolution and it was the Commissioner or Sub-Commissioner who would normally provide it in an informal decision and without written records. Their decisions were invariably accepted very well in New South Wales, which speaks to the good-standing that the Gold Commissioners held in that State by comparison to the despised, high-handed attitudes and behaviours of the Gold Commissioners on the Victorian goldfields (Hamilton, 2014).

Although Victoria, after separation from New South Wales in 1851, had inherited or copied much of the same legislation and procedures as were already being used in New South Wales, Lieutenant-Governor Charles La Trobe in Victoria prioritised the revenue raising functions of the Commissioners over the need to preserve law and order. We will confine ourselves, in this instance, to a discussion of how the Gold Commissioner system was applied in New South Wales in the early days of gold rushes such as at Tooloom from 1859 onwards.

The Assistant Gold Commissioner at Timbarra reported to the Gold Commissioner in Charge of Crown Lands for the Northern Gold District. George Green Emmett, for example, was appointed from the 1st of June 1859 as Sub-Commissioner at Timbarra and then as Assistant Gold Commissioner atTimbarra. He became Assistant Commissioner (2nd Class) in 1864. He was appointed to be:

> *A magistrate of the territory and its dependencies, and officer responsible for determining the extent and position of claims and marking their extent. (The Sydney Morning Herald, 4th of June 1859).*

The Gold Commissioner not only had the task of marking out the miners' claims on the goldfields, he also was the Administrator who had the responsibility for collecting the hated Miner's Licence Fee. To enforce this, he had the assistance of a number of mounted troopers and foot-soldiers. Some of these would have been Indigenous men who were usually highly valued for their tracking ability. Bushrangers were a constant threat on most goldfields in New South Wales in the 1850s.

The gold escort service:

From mid-1859, a public gold-escort had been organised by the local Gold Sub-Commissioner to take gold from Timbarra and McLeods Creek to Grafton from whence it then went to Sydney by coastal-steamer. This service had been extended to Tooloom and Pretty Gully as well by the end of that year. This arrangement has made it difficult, however, to estimate the output from the Tooloom goldfield at this time, for gold from Tooloom was then included in the total gold output of all these fields. Many of the miners had, however, family links to Ipswich in Queensland and most preferred to send their gold there via a newly established, private gold escort instead of using the public gold escort service at Grafton.

Well travelled roads to and between the New South Wales goldfields were often in a very rough state due to heavy dray traffic and the passage of the gold escort's members was, thus, not only dangerous but it was also a very uncomfortable ride. Despite being heavily armed, the members of the gold escort (usually ex-police or military men) had to avoid the comforts of any inns along their routes in order to deprive the bushrangers or their agents from gaining any useful intelligence about the strength of their gold escort or about the amount of gold that they were transporting to the Sydney Mint.

The gold miners in both New South Wales and Victoria hated the mining licence fee for they believed that it unfairly penalised all miners, whether they had already found gold or not. In Victoria, this was just another grudge added to the long list of grievances already held against the brutal collectors of the licence fee. In New South Wales, the miners held no such grudge against the Commissioners and their decisions but, instead, blamed the unfair 'System' for this despised tax on their labours. This positive attitude can be seen in the small grievance that had been raised in the following report on the Tooloom goldfields by a somewhat disgruntled digger.

The *Clarence and Richmond Examiner*

Poverty Point Diggings,

18th of July 1859. From our own correspondent.

> *The Tooloom diggings have turned out very unsatisfactory to the great number of miners who rushed there. They return to the Timbarra daily (in groups of) forties and fifties and those old diggings have now been more appreciated than ever and they yield a golden harvest to the industrious and steady miner. Mr Austin, the agent of the Bank of New South Wales, sent 2200 ounces via Armidale and Maitland and 400 ounces were sent by private persons thus making a total of 2600 ounces. Captain Scott and the new gold escort arrived two or three days afterwards and nearly 1200 ounces were sent down to Grafton by the new line of road to meet the 'Grafton Steamer'. By the next escort, we expect to send away a still larger quantity.*
>
> *Mr Emmett - the Commissioner, has been successful enough to judge satisfactorily upon all the conflicting claims here. He has also issued a notice prohibiting the opening of stores and public houses on the Sabbath day. It is a great pity that none of our religious bodies deem it necessary to have divine worship celebrated here occasionally. There is estimated to be about two thousand miners on the Timbarra diggings and, with the exception of a flying visit from a Roman Catholic clergyman, there has been no notice taken of us.*

Mr Emmett - the Timbarra Sub-Commissioner, did not seem to have attracted any of the miners' ire about his own activities in this small report above in the *Clarence and Richmond* newspaper. Emmett's decisions seem to have been well-tolerated rather than being reviled as would most likely have occurred in Victoria at this time.

Mr G W F Addison was appointed Sub-Commissioner at Tooloom, Bingara, Rocky River and Uralla and, eventually, Chief Gold Commissioner, Northern Goldfields. After the Gold

Commissioner System was abolished in NSW, Addison later became a Stipendiary Magistrate in Sydney in January 1882 before retiring voluntarily in 1899.

A letter of appreciation to Commissioner Addison:

Mr Addison, as the Northern Gold Commissioner, was based at Nundle. He also had a house in the Tenterfield area in the vicinity of the Bruxner Highway to Casino. He was assisted by Mr Emmett the Sub-Commissioner who was based at Timbarra.

To G.W.F. Addison, Esq, Gold Commissioner,

> *Tooloom - Sir, - We, the undersigned publicans, storekeepers, miners, and others resident on Upper and Lower Tooloom and Pretty Gully beg to record our unqualified approbation at the pleasing and satisfactory manner in which you have discharged your duties as Commissioner and Magistrate during your residence on these goldfields. We also attribute to your intelligence and activity, the general peace and good order that we have enjoyed. It is, moreover, our opinion that all cases of dispute and adjudication have been most satisfactorily disposed of with the kind and gentlemanly conduct, which has at all times, characterised your intercourse with the resident population.*
>
> *In conclusion, we beg to offer our warmest wishes for your future welfare and express our hope that your stay amongst us may be long continued and our interests be correspondingly advanced.*

We are, Sir, your obedient servants.

The table below is a brief summary of the numbers and types of signatories to this previous letter. For those readers who are interested, please see the Appendices for a complete list of their names and their occupations. It is fair to assume from the high number of signatories to this letter that most miners were quite satisfied with the services provided by the Gold Commissioner Mr Addison across these northern Clarence River goldfields. The discoverer of Tooloom goldfield - James Perkins, as well as William May, were both signatories.

153 persons signed this above letter. 3 of these did not indicate their occupations. Of the remainder:
126 Miners signed the letter.
13 Storekeepers signed the letter and so did 5 innkeepers or publicans.
4 butchers signed and so did 3 administrators, including the local Postmaster.
2 tradesmen (1 blacksmith and 1 shoe-maker) signed; and
1 Bullock driver also signed the above letter.

Table 3. Signatories by occupation, to the letter of appreciation to Gold Commissioner Addison.

The hated Miner's Licence Fee:

Governor Fitzroy and Colonial Secretary Thompson in New South Wales had both realised from the beginning of the official gold rush to Ophir near Bathurst that the maintenance of public law and order required funding; they thus moved quickly to assert the Crown's right to ownership of the gold resources by imposing a license fee on all would-be gold miners. This licence fee not only gave the miner the right to peg out an area of eight feet (2.4 metres) square as his claim, but also, it enabled the colonial governments of both New South Wales and Victoria to raise revenues to provide policing and administration. It was also hoped that the fee of 30 shillings a month would be an effective disincentive to persuade critically-needed workers in Sydney and Melbourne from abandoning their employers to rush off to the new goldfields. The issuing of these gold licences also enabled the Colonial Government to keep track of the numbers of persons on the different gold fields around New South Wales as to who would need the provision of public services (Serle,1963 and Ward,1966).

The licence fee was a major source of complaint by miners in both New South Wales and Victoria although it was downgraded to 10 shillings a month in New South Wales in 1853 after near riots on the Turon. Victoria followed this lead of New South Wales sometime later. Despite this concession, the state of the roads to the goldfields remained an ongoing issue for the miners in New South Wales. The miners felt that they were not getting enough spent on them out of this onerous 'Tax'. The licence fee was finally abolished in 1855 in Victoria following the 'Eureka Stockade' incident and it was replaced in that Colony by a 'Miner's Right' costing 10 shillings per annum; the holder of a Miner's Right was also given the right to vote.

This provision of 'the Right to Vote' to the holder of a miner's right in both Colonies was a very significant change for, up until 1855, only the squatters (equivalent to the landed gentry of the old world) had possessed this right and, as a result, political power had thus just passed into the eager hands of the miners and of the new middle class and was based on this new found mining wealth. Democracy had now arrived in Australia curtesy of this new mining wealth!

Over a quarter of an ounce of Clarence River gold, for a day's effort
Source: Garry Gatfield, 2024

A duty on gold exports partially replaced the Miner's Licence Fee in 1855:

An export duty of 2s 6d per ounce of gold was also levied on gold exports in Victoria in 1855 in an effort to compensate for the lost licence fee revenues. New South Wales then adopted both changes in 1857 (Carrington, 1960 and Crowley, 1980).

There was an unintended consequence of these developments in December 1859. The new Colony of Queensland then found itself at a disadvantage relative to New South Wales and Victoria. Queensland laws remained the laws of New South Wales as they were in 1855 and miners, gold buyers and gold-related businessmen in the new Colony of Queensland then became quite vociferous in their effects to have the gold duty laws revised for them as newspaper articles of the time demonstrated.

Report on a Brisbane meeting about the vexing duty on gold exports:

From *The Moreton Bay Courier*

24th of January 1860.

A meeting of the representatives of the commercial interests of Brisbane was held in the Exchange Rooms, Brisbane, yesterday at noon, Jas. Gibbon, Esq., in the chair.

The Chairman, in opening the proceedings of the meeting said that they were met together to consider the injurious effects of the export duty on gold on the trading community of Brisbane and to the interests of the Colony generally and to devise means to remedy that which appeared to militate against the welfare of all classes.

The export duty on gold was of great import to them in their present position as it would cause the gold from Tooloom to be sent via Grafton where it necessitated a double duty; there being not only the duty payable at the ports in Queensland but a further duty, which would be charged before it was received into the Sydney mint. Acting injuriously, as he conceived it was and against the interest of the place, he considered it their duty to do all that they could to remedy this evil.

Mr. G. Harris moved the first resolution as follows:- 'That this meeting has met to represent the mercantile and trading interests of the Brisbane view to regret the imposition of a tax of 2s. 6d. per oz on gold exported from Queensland and to desire a speedy abolition of the same, as it interferes materially with our commercial operation with the goldfields at Tooloom and with its neighbourhood.

Capt. R. J. Coley seconded the resolution and cited, in illustration of the necessity for action, that the owners of the nugget, which had been inappropriately called the 'Lady Bowen Nugget' were determined to send it (to Sydney) by way of Grafton.

Mr. Harris corroborated the statement of Capt. Coley. He had been in treaty for the purchase of the nugget in question, but the business had been prevented from being brought to a successful issue in consequence of the (gold) export duty.

Mr. R. Cribb moved, and Mr. Heussler seconded the second resolution – 'That with a view to the speedy abolition of this tax upon gold, this meeting authorises the Chairman of the Brisbane Exchange Rooms to prepare and forward to the Executive Government of this Colony, a memorial signed by him (the Chairman) on behalf of the mercantile community of this city, praying that the said obnoxious tax may be suspended until the meeting of the Legislature.

Moved by Mr. Cribb and seconded by Mr. Dowse - That the following gentlemen should form a sub-committee to assist the Chairman to draw up the memorial; Messrs. Bartley, Cribb and Brookes were named. It was afterwards decided that the Chairman should wait upon the Governor, accompanied by Messrs. Bartley and Harris, so that his Excellency might be made aware of the injurious effects upon trade arising from the duty, should he be desirous of making inquiries of a commercial character.

The Gold Commissioners role in public safety:

After the Gold Commissioners had been appointed to a gold district, they were given the help of gold police. At Timbarra in 1858, this took the form of a corporal and a trooper who then lived on the goldfield and these were then assisted in turn by mounted regular police as required. Their role involved providing mounted police and foot police and they all helped to support the authority of the Gold Commissioner in mining matters rather than just having to carry out normal police duties (Wilkinson, 1980: 61-62).

Another of the roles of the New South Wales Gold Commissioners and his assisting Sub-Commissioners was to organise the safe passage of the digger's gold from the goldfields of the Colony to the Sydney Mint.

A murderous event on the Clermont Goldfield in Central Queensland:

In 1867, the new Colony of Queensland was shocked by a report of the murders of two young policemen doing gold-escort duties from Rockhampton to Clermont. Constables Powell and Cahill were part of the gold-escort with Sergeant Julian in charge but, this time, the escort had an additional member in John Thomas Griffin - the Rockhampton Gold Commissioner, who had previously been the Police Magistrate at Clermont. Soon after departing from Rockhampton, Sergeant Julian had accused Griffith of trying to poison him and angrily refused to go any further. This left Constables Power and Cahill to continue with Griffin with a large consignment of bullion and bank notes for Clermont. On reaching Clermont, Griffith took a room at a local inn whilst the two constables set up their camp on the banks of the MacKenzie River. The next day, Griffith set off to return to Rockhampton but without saying goodbye to the two troopers at the Mackenzie River Crossing.

Several days later, a bushman found the dead bodies of Powell and Cahill in their camp; they appeared to have been shot in the head. A police party immediately left Rockhampton for Clermont. This party included several police detectives plus Sergeant Julian of the gold escort, the bank manager – Mr Hall, the police doctor and Mr Thomas Griffith – the local Gold Commissioner. After Dr. Salmon examined the bodies, he declared that they had been first sedated before being shot in the head and, after the police gathered further evidence at the crime scene, John Thomas Griffith immediately became the prime suspect.

Once the police learned of Griffith's gambling debts, he was soon arrested and charged with Constable Power's and Cahill's murders. His trial began on the 16th of March, 1868 and, despite his vigorous claim of innocence, the jury found him guilty of murder; he was sentenced to death and was hanged at the Old Rockhampton Jail on the 1st of June, 1868.

(Source: The Police Museum, Qld.)

The role of a gold escort member was a dangerous one:

Between 1862 and 1867, bushrangers killed 20 men and 20 police were wounded; during the same period, 23 bushrangers were killed or hanged.

(Source: Education Services and National Library of Australia, 2013)

The gold-escorts were prime targets for attacks by bushrangers because they regularly carried large amounts of gold and notes to and from the goldfields and to the Sydney Mint. One of the largest heists by bushrangers in New South Wales 'gold rush' history was carried out at Eugowra Rocks on the Forbes to Sydney gold-escort service via Orange in June 1862. Forbes was then the chief hub for the Lachlan Fold Belt's gold mining in the southern part of the New England Orogen (a mountain-building zone).

This 1862 heist netted the bushranging gang led by Frank Gardiner, gold and notes valued at approximately fourteen thousand pounds. This was an enormous amount in those days but, unfortunately for them, Gardiner and his young men had missed the same escort's thirty-four thousand pounds worth of gold and notes, the week before. Despite initially fleeing to Queensland, Gardiner was arrested, charged and then jailed on the 8th of July 1864. He was pardoned ten years later in July 1874 and left Australia to keep a saloon in San Francisco for the remaining years of his life (Jones, 2000). The miners around Fairfield (Drake), Timbarra and the new areas such as Tooloom to the north of these on the Clarence River were rarely troubled by bushrangers but they were certainly aware of their potential presence in their areas; if gold was lost in an attack on the gold escort, the miners lost all of their 'pile' without any hope of compensation.

In the first letters of the 'Trip to the diggings' by the *Moreton Bay Courier's 'Special Correspondent',* it is quite difficult to discern just how significant the Tooloom goldfield actually was in terms of gold production. Many diggers preferred to take their own gold down to Ipswich themselves but these usually adopted a despondent or negative air and cautioned anyone else from trying their luck at Tooloom. Not all were fooled.

There were reports of nuggets in various letters from the Tooloom goldfields. However, many of the miners on this and on other fields preferred to keep details of their finds to themself for reasons of personal safety.

The historic former Tooloom Hotel built by John Payne, now a renovated B&B
Source: Garry Gatfield, 2024

6

Early inter-colonial rivalry

The following report reached *The Moreton Bay Courier* in early June 1859, via Grafton. It is obviously written by a southerner, but his criticism of the lack of *enterprise* of the Brisbane and Ipswich colonials was probably warranted:

The Timbarra goldfields are extending daily and the population is steadily increasing. They have never met a check from the first. The dry season has been very favourable for their development and has enabled the carriers to keep them well supplied with all the necessaries of life at a moderate rate. I understand that good diggings have been discovered at Tooloom - some thirty miles nearer to Brisbane and just midway between Grafton and Ipswich. This will enable the northern metropolis to participate in the trade, the distance being little more than one hundred miles from Ipswich.

There appears to be a great want of energy and enterprise among your people. If they had opened a road from Tooloom to Fairfield, the distance to McLeod's Creek would not have been more than 160 to 170 miles and would be quite practicable but, of course, it would involve some trouble and expense.

The Grafton Road Committee have fulfilled their pledge to raise and to expend £300 in opening their new line of road and several teams are now travelling upon it and carrying 50 cwt. each trip, which usually occupies ten days in going. It is also understood that the Government has determined to place an escort on the line immediately; the distance for horsemen is now only seventy miles and it is confidently hoped that a dray road will, ere long, be made in that distance.

The road has been surveyed by order of the Government and approved and a grant of money is hourly expected from them for its improvement. Owing to the exorbitant charge made by the Grafton Steamer Company for the conveyance of gold, very little is sent on freight and, consequently, the bulk is never reported It is, however, certain that from 500 to 800 ounces are sent every trip and that a very large proportion of the gold reported by the northern escort is sent from Timbarra along the table-land and is reported as Rocky River gold (Uralla), whilst it is known that the Armidale fields are almost deserted. It has been the policy of all parties connected with the Timbarra to avoid puffing and to conceal everything as much as possible.

As the young goldfield of Tooloom developed in late 1859, there was an outbreak of all sorts of inter-colonial rivalry as well as border disputes, taxation issues, road building, deception and secrecy. We will see later in our story how the Colonial Government in Sydney suddenly switched the public gold-escort from Grafton to Maitland at the end of 1859 to the indignation of many of the locals at Grafton and on the Clarence goldfields. We of Queensland also previously saw how the Colonial Government in Sydney arbitrarily redefined its northern border with Queensland by using *The Australian Colonies Act*, thus shifting it northwards to follow the line of the MacPherson Ranges at Latitude 26° S. This destroyed the new Colony's hopes of keeping the Tooloom goldfield within the border.

Despite knowing that Separation was due to happen in late 1859, it also seemed to be a little suspicious that the Sydney Colonial government would decide to hold a general election in the first half of 1859, which meant that the large mining electorate of North Goldfields, which included Canoona in Queensland as well as Tooloom and Timbarra in northern New South Wales, would be affected by this decision. It was even more suspicious when the ballot papers from Canoona mysteriously disappeared so that Queensland had to reschedule its election for that part of the electorate that was left to the north of the New South Wales - Queensland border. Even if such events were only petty annoyances, these incidents did serve to stoke interstate rivalry from the beginning and one can claim that this is still experienced today in the ferocious rivalry of 'State of Origin' football matches.

A private gold-escort from Tooloom to Ipswich:

At the end of August 1859, the citizens of Ipswich had excitedly gathered to farewell the first private gold escort to depart from that town for the Tooloom diggings. This expedition was led by Mr Ranken, J.P. and he was supported by two mounted and armed constables with four men leading pack-horses. Mr Maughan from the Bank of Australasia also accompanied the party (The Herald, 30th of August 1859).

A public meeting in Ipswich followed after the return of this private gold-escort from Tooloom. The escort had completed the return journey from Tooloom to Ipswich in only twenty-eight hours and this was sooner than expected; the escort also claimed that a slight alteration in their route would have reduced that time and would have made the distance to Tooloom from Ipswich only about seventy miles.

The Maitland Mercury and Hunter River General Advertiser

From the Tooloom Diggings

22nd of September 1859

Report on the Tooloom Gold Escort from the Herald's Brisbane Correspondent:

The escort brought down one hundred and eighty ounces and the smallness of that quantity is accounted for from the fact that the Grafton escort had just left Tooloom, as also had an agent of one of the banks with a considerable quantity of gold in his possession, which he had purchased on the ground. The escort has again departed and the quantity next brought down will probably enable us to form a pretty accurate conclusion as to the real productiveness of the Tooloom gold-field.

The diggers of Tooloom have expressed themselves anxious to see a regular communication opened up with Moreton Bay. The journey from Grafton is tedious and difficult, especially for drays, on account of the number of creeks to cross. The stores thence obtained were consequently expensive and were irregularly supplied. Complaints were also rife as to the quality of the goods sent up and, especially, of the flour.

When the Ipswich escort was at Tooloom, rations were extremely scarce and, indeed, were unprocurable with the exception of meat, which was plentiful enough so, as soon as the return of the escort made this fact known, several drayloads of provisions were immediately despatched from Ipswich so that the necessities of the diggers would speedily be relieved ... I may also mention that a person belonging to the escort brought down a specimen of coal, which he had procured on the diggings and he stated that the diggers told him that this mineral was plentiful there. I do not pretend to any knowledge of these things, but I had always understood that gold and coal were never found in close proximity or in similar geological formations. I do believe that I had formerly stated that Tooloom was situated on the Queensland side of the boundary line as it is proposed to be drawn and this continues to be the opinion of some people here. Further enquiries have led me now to think that this is, however, incorrect and that the diggings are in the territory of New South Wales.

Further extracts of these reports of the Tooloom goldfield to a public meeting in Ipswich are included below:

The Northern Australian

13th of September 1859

Mr Ranken: As this meeting was aware, the gold-escort had left (Ipswich) on the Wednesday and were three days and some hours before reaching the diggings. On arrival there, he had told the diggers that the private escort had been formed to open communications with Ipswich and that they expected to be supported. The diggers answered that they would send their gold by the escort and hoped that they should receive some provisions from Ipswich since, with the exception of beef, there was scarcely a day's provision on the diggings. They had sent one hundred and eighty ounces (of gold) down by the escort as a trial, but this amount was not to be considered as any test of the quantity of gold on the diggings; he had seen besides that about 300 ounces and, as they would be aware, a man does not usually let his neighbour know what he may have in his possession.

He had met with a man with whom he was well acquainted who had 250 ounces and another who had 600 ounces. To show what had been done on the diggings, one man – the one who had got the 41 oz. nugget – had 40 lbs weight of gold, and another had made £1300. He further noted that his audience should bear in mind that the diggings had not been opened for more than four months.'

The Chairman then enquired if Mr Ranken had any idea of the number of diggers on the ground? Mr Ranken replied that he could not form an estimate, as they were so scattered. Mr Maurice thought there were more than 500 and that there were 100 more expected to arrive on the day that the escort left Tooloom. Mr Ranken was at a loss to know where they would get provisions; many had already left the diggings after being unable to get them.

The gold at Tooloom was procured at a depth of two foot and the digging was principally along the creek. Deep sinking had not been tried to any extent for the diggers were perfectly satisfied with their present earnings. They were well off for water, as there was a creek through the diggings with holes in it that were twenty feet deep. The ground was so broken that diggers had to carry their washing stuff in bags to the water. A dray could not travel on the ground and it would be difficult to carry the earth even with the assistance of a pack-horse.

In answer to a question concerning the road, Mr Ranken said he considered the road to be tolerably good, with the exception of two or three bad pinches; bullock drays would thus be able to take two tons each if they travelled in company to allow them to double-bank at the bad places.

The worst creek that they had to cross could be made good at a small expense. He considered the distance to be from 92 to 95 miles. The stock feed from Balbi's to the Nine-Mile Station was very bad but after the Nine-Mile Station was passed, there was an abundance of good grass and water.

The Chairman then requested Mr Maughan to address the meeting:

Mr Maughan said they had rested on the Sunday after arriving on the diggings; on Monday, he went to see Joe's Gully over a devil of a hill, which had required good lungs and legs. When he got there, he saw different parties at work, and asked them to show him their gold, which they did. One man who they called Black Dan had a 14 oz. nugget. It was the same man who had found the 16 oz. nugget that was shown in Mr Given's window. The men were at work at daybreak but he was confident from what he saw there that the diggings were good. He had also gone with Mr. Maurice (as there was scarcely any goods left in the store) to see the new rush; he had spoken there to a party of about seven Scotch and four Englishmen; they said they were doing well, but they were working with their toes peeping out from their boots, as there were no boots to be had. He had no doubt but that if more stores had been previously sent up, that instead of 180 ozs they might have brought down 1800 oz.

The Northern Australian newspaper added the following:

Tooloom: – The excitement caused by the reports of this gold-field, which were brought by the gold-escort, is evidenced by the migration of large numbers of our population; nearly 200 left during the past week. Mr Fleming is forwarding a large supply of freshly-ground flour from his mills and Messrs. Panton and G. H. Wilson and Co. have despatched a large quantity of supplies. Seventeen drays have been forwarded by these parties since Wednesday last. Mr Maughan, in addition to the information that he gave to the meeting, mentioned that the diggers can also find a quantity of black sand with the gold, which is valued at 15s. per ounce.

A new route for the Grafton gold-escort after the Separation:

Considerable rivalry soon developed between the Ipswich private gold-escort to Tooloom and the New South Wales public gold-escort to Grafton. After the separation of Queensland from New South Wales and upon the commissioning of Sir George Ferguson Bowen on the 6th of June 1859, the border between the two Colonies had still to be determined. The New South Wales Colonial Office had a surprise in store for both Grafton and Ipswich and, in December 1859, had not only re-defined its north-eastern border but had also announced a new route for the official gold-escort service that saw the gold from the Timbarra and the Tooloom areas shipped to Sydney via Maitland instead of via Grafton by steamer.

The Sydney Morning Herald

1st of December 1859

From a Correspondent who reported that:

A public meeting was recently held in Grafton to discuss the unexpected change to the existing route of the gold-escort to Grafton from the Clarence goldfields; this meeting concerned a recent diversion of the service to Sydney via Armidale and Maitland.

The Colonial Secretary had just been asked to justify this change by a Mr Clark Irving. A long letter from Captain Scott was read out at this meeting that stated that the Government had agreed that it was advisable to send it to Maitland via Armidale; Capt. Scott outlined his objections to a Grafton route by saying that the road to Grafton was over a difficult and rocky mountain route where there was a lack of accommodation and that this had meant that the men of the Grafton escort had to camp out and to either hobble or tether their horses each evening.

Captain Scott further claimed that there was also the risk of encountering dangerous floods in the Clarence River.

This meeting of Grafton residents angrily refuted the former claim of a lack of accommodation by pointing out that:

This is distinctly shown to be incorrect, as at short stages, varying from fifteen to twenty-five miles along the Grafton line, ample accommodation, both for the men and the horses, has always been provided.

The Grafton residents also further argued that:

- *their weekly steamer service to Sydney via the Port of Grafton was the legitimate outlet for their produce, including their Clarence area gold*
- *that Grafton was a much shorter distance (being no more than 60 to 100 miles) from all the Clarence gold fields by comparison to Armidale's 140 to 200 miles distance away and that:*

The great danger of crossing the Clarence was a myth; the crossing-place was a shingly flat, wide enough for several drays to cross abreast and, that the gold-escort had never been detained for a single moment, whilst there are deep fords on the Maitland line, and men and horses have been frequently drowned.

The Grafton residents' petition to the Colonial Secretary on the Wednesday before this article was published may also well have added that:

There also seems to be less bushranger activity in this Clarence area by comparison to the New England area from Armidale down to Tamworth.

If the residents of Grafton had added this last thought, they would have been very prescient as the Eugowra gold heist on Sunday the 15th of June 1862 showed. Their pleas remained unanswered by the New South Wales Colonial Secretary and, given the earlier story about the final position of the Queensland-New South Wales borderline, this certainly makes this author suspect that the New South Wales Colonial administration never had any intention of conceding the then 'lucrative' Tooloom goldfield to Queensland.

Sir George Bowen met the Governor General in Sydney to advise him that he was taking over the Governorship for Queensland after Separation was proclaimed. Bowen and his family then sailed from Sydney, arriving in Moreton Bay on the 10th of December 1859, which thus became the official date of Separation from the Colony of New South Wales.

Thieves on the Diggings:

Petty thievery was also reported on the Tooloom goldfield in 1859 as the following excerpt from the letters of the 'Special Correspondent' shows.

From: The Moreton Bay Courier

By the 'Special Correspondent'

From Tooloom Creek: 6th Of September 1859

We have been troubled with some unpleasant customers here lately, who find it easier to steal gold from others than to work for it themselves. Ten ounces of gold and a watch was stolen from a hut last week; last night a man had his pocket cut open and a ten-ounce nugget taken from it, and to-day. a man found himself minus his saddle. There are no police here at present.

The Gold Commissioner did his best to keep law and order but getting around his domain was difficult at the best of times.

Fine alluvial gold from the Clarence River
Source: Garry Gatfield, 2024

7

Difflo's Nugget

This next story relates the sad case of Charles Difflo and his 80 oz nugget Court case. The Court had ruled in October 1859, that Difflo's big nugget find in Tooloom Creek opposite Joe's Gully should be surrendered to safe custody whilst awaiting a legal determination of the correct ownership of his nugget. Difflo refused to surrender the nugget and hid it. He was later sued in the Queensland Supreme Court (in Equity) by his previous two partners in their claim and this cost him more than the large nugget was worth. News of this find was quickly reported in various newspapers including the following:

From *The Moreton Bay Courier*

15th October, 1859.

A large nugget!

There are reports that a nugget weighing 8 lbs has been found at the Queensland diggings. We were visited yesterday by a person who had seen the receipt from the authority to whom the nugget had been entrusted by the digger for safe conveyance; we have also heard from Ipswich that the tale of the large nugget had been told there in truthful words. We have also heard that those who consider that they have a right to equal shares with the finder have made their appearance in the sister town. Up to the present time, the evidence is in favour of the nugget, but as we seek not to cause a rush, we prefer waiting for further particulars before affixing our belief to this rumour.

The Sydney Morning Herald

Queensland. 25th of October 1859.

Ipswich Herald, 17th instant.

Several parties have arrived in Ipswich from the Tooloom diggings this week and give expression to opinions in accordance with the majority - that there is plenty of gold there but they are still short of water. At the beginning of the last week, there was a new rush to a gully about twenty miles from the old working ground (Pretty Gully). *Mr Betts also brought down this week about 250 ozs of gold and, amongst it, was a fine specimen of a nugget, which weighed 80 oz 16 dwt 6 grs. This was obtained by a German (Charles Difflo) who had not been long on the diggings but there is still a dispute about its rightful ownership.*

The *Moreton Bay Courier* of the 19th of October also published a letter from Tooloom relating to this nugget and bearing the signature of W. O'Donnell in which the writer says:

> *There are many heavy nuggets being found here. I had one in my hand yesterday evening weighing 6lbs some ounces* (6 troy lbs 8 oz); *one was a solid mass of gold free from any quartz. It was found by an old German and was shown to me by Mr Panton's partner in whose custody it was for safe-keeping.*
>
> *I have great hopes for the claim in which I am working but we are only just getting it into working order. It is paying very well in the meantime, although we are in the worst part, for we have prospected it all over. We are now getting from £4 to £5 per week, but our average for six months will be above £16 per week and that is without any heavy find. We are not one hundred paces from where the 80oz nugget was found and we are close to where many other nuggets were found in the same vicinity.*

The gold nugget mentioned in the above letter was the 80oz nugget of Charles Difflo. Two previous partners in his claim had disputed his sole ownership of the same. This Difflo Nugget dispute ended up in the Court system where the value of many a large nugget was often lost in legal fees due to ex-claim holders seeking their share, (rightfully or otherwise). This is one reason why the diggers were always keen to sell their big nuggets quickly, so that they could convert their hard-won golden gains to ready cash. The miners could have made better money by exhibiting the nuggets for a fee; this had been pointed out to them by an earlier correspondent in 1851 after Kerr's hundredweight of gold-laced quartz specimen was discovered. This advice fell on deaf ears, and most of these valuable historic treasures (nuggets) were lost to either the Sydney, Melbourne or English Mints.

This German migrant known as Charles Difflo found his 80oz plus nugget in Joe's Gully at Tooloom in September 1859, not far from where the Lady Bowen Nugget was found a short time later. The ensuing Court case was well-documented and these documents will now be employed to give the reader a comprehensive understanding of how such proceedings would be initiated and handled by the Gold Commissioner System in New South Wales and of the serious consequences of such proceedings for the unfortunate miner if these progressed to a higher Court in the New South Wales legal system.

The Supreme Court Case of Charles Difflo:

From *The Moreton Bay Courier (19th of October 1859, Brisbane).*

In the Supreme Court of New South Wales, Moreton Bay.

Before his Honour Mr. Justice Lutwyche.

Kyezor and another V. Difflo. - In Equity.

The trial commenced with the plaintiff's Counsel – Mr Lilley, applying for an injunction to stop the defendant from selling or disposing of his large gold nugget.

An injunction was duly granted to restrain the defendant and associates from disposing or selling of his nugget of gold. Kyezor, Lifleur, and Difflo had all been partners in a claim on the Tooloom gold fields.

Kyezor related how two of the party had gone off prospecting in September, leaving Difflo in charge of their digging. On their return, they discovered that Difflo had found the latter nugget and had sold the claim and tools before then making his way back to Ipswich to await the return of the gold-escort with his prize. Difflo had subsequently refused to give any account to his partners or to surrender their portion of that prize to them.

Brisbane Supreme Court (Tuesday 19th of May 1860).

The Sittings of the Court for the trial of the Civil case resumed.

Kyezor and Another V. (Charles) Difflo.

> *The issue directed by his Honour in the exercise of his equity jurisdiction, was referred to a jury for their opinion upon a matter of fact. This was the question - did the erstwhile partnership still exist when the nugget was found? The plaintiffs - Philip Kyezor and Albert Lifleur, both claimed partnership in the defendant's nugget and that this partnership was ongoing. Charles Difflo denied that the partnership still existed. The formation of a partnership was admitted, so the only questions to be decided by the jury were, whether the partnership entered into was dissolved on the 27th day of September 1859 or at any subsequent date and, if so, when?*

The defendant remained in custody; this was for contempt of an order of the Court to deliver up the nugget in his possession pending legal proceedings. Charles Difflo, although informed that his appearance in Court could be procured by a writ of Habeas Corpus, was not present and nor was he represented by Counsel.

Mr Blakeney appeared for the plaintiffs and proceeded to examine Philip Kyezor, whose, evidence was to the following effect:

> *In August, the witness (and plaintiff) had been a gold miner at Tooloom on his own claim, which he had taken possession of in the previous April. At the end of August, he had been joined by Albert Lifleur and Charles Difflo (the defendant) and had been working with them for one month on terms of equal shares in any gold found; this arrangement had then continued for a further month.*
>
> *Kyezor claimed he'd had occasion to visit the Gold Commissioner and, on his return, had informed his partners that he believed himself to have discovered gold in a place twenty miles away. The witness then further claimed that it was decided that he and one other of them should be chosen by lot to go to work on the new claim, whilst Difflo remained on the Tooloom gold field to work on their pre-existing claim.*
>
> *The lot fell on Kyezor; he and Lifleur then departed for the new rush sometime between the 15th and the 18th of September after agreeing to maintain the agreement for the division of the gold found on the original claim and to apply that agreement to the new claim as well. The witness*

further argued that there was still shared gold (afterwards sold for£21) left in the communal gold bag on the original claim and that all the original tools had also been left behind there along with eight days of rations; this latter had belonged to Kyezor alone.

The witness claimed to have remained three days at the new rush before returning for the tools. He then returned alone to the old claim with the purpose of retrieving these. He further recalled that he then spent a further two days working with Charles Difflo at the old claim before returning to his companion Lifleur after a one day's journey. Kyezor also recalled remaining at the new rush for one further day before returning to the old claim to bring clothes and intending to return with Difflo to the new rush.

Before he reached the old claim, however, he had found an intoxicated Difflo in a lodging house in Tooloom. He recalled that he had expressed astonishment at seeing him and was informed by the latter that he had been very lucky, having found a nugget of 82 ounces. Difflo further informed him that he had sold the claim, the tools, tent and all, and had enough to live on. Witness then said that he had told Difflo that he was not content with what had been done; they must have a proper settlement. Difflo had refused to give this witness anything. Witness, in consequence, then endeavoured to find a magistrate but without success.

Witness then threatened to bring an action against the defendant. Since that time, he had never received anything from the defendant. The old claim had been occupied, and he'd never recovered possession of it again......

Mr Lilley then stated in evidence that he had been instructed to take legal proceedings by both Kyezor and Lifleur. The latter could not, at the time he'd left Brisbane, have been aware that the present issue was about to be tried. The depositions of Difflo's evidence, as taken before the Master in Equity, were then read and His Honour proceeded to sum up, commenting upon the discrepancies in Difflo's evidence, as to the nugget being found on the Monday or Tuesday after the Sunday on which Kyezor had left and, in another, that it had not been found until a week or more after Kyezor's departure.

The Difflo Verdict:

The jury returned a verdict to the effect that the partnership was not dissolved on the 27th of September and stating also that there was no evidence to show that the partnership had since been dissolved.

The Weekly Epitome

In the *Moreton Bay Courier (19th May, 1860)*

In the important case of Kyezor and Another v. Difflo.

The verdict of the jury in favour of the plaintiffs established the right of the plaintiffs to a share in the Difflo Nugget. Difflo refused to hand over the nugget (claiming to have forgotten where he'd hid it) or to share the proceeds of its sale with his former mates so he was immediately sentenced to detention for 'Contempt of Court'.

Difflo's Attorney stated his case:

From: *The Moreton Bay Courier* (Brisbane, Qld.)

(5th of September 1861).

Letters to the Editor.

Re: Difflo's Case.

Sir, - The case of Charles Difflo involving as it does, according to your leading article on the subject, a principle affecting the liberty of the person, would be a valuable thesis were the true facts of the case warrant any deserved sympathy for an unfortunate victim of chancery. This man, although a British subject under the permanent care of Mr Sneyd and a pensioner on the public purse is, however, a very vulgar martyr.

This case, stripped of its outer texture, and laid bare in its naked simplicity, merely brings to view another instance of the greed for gold, creating in a human being a desire of possession so strong as to subdue the sweets of liberty itself ...

I am not going to argue the policy of the law in question, or to suggest a remedy; this I leave to the legal members of the parliament; but, as Attorney for Charles Difflo in the suit and without violating any professional rules, I can correct the impression you seem to have formed on the apparent hardship of his case; arising, as you put it, from his misfortune in having lost the nugget. Now, did I believe this, or did the Attorneys for the plaintiff believe this, I am sure all parties would willingly consent to his release; but as we know the contrary to be the fact and it can be proved, then there are no grounds for sympathy. Were Difflo to be let out to-morrow, the proceeds of that nugget would soon be in his pocket in the shape of Australian bank notes.

I saw the nugget but a few days before he was arrested and advised him to lodge it with the Court according to the Court order. The jury returned a verdict to the effect that the partnership was not dissolved on the 27th of September and stated that there was no evidence to show that the partnership had since been dissolved. Had he done so, this cause would have ended long ago and he would have been spared eighteen months imprisonment. He refused, and an order was issued for his arrest. I am informed by the Sheriff's Officer that, when Difflo was arrested, the nugget was on the table in his house, and had the officer the power, he could have seized it; the officer was instead directed to arrest this person only for contempt of court. He could not touch the nugget. Difflo addressed some words to his wife and son who were present (in German) with reference, no doubt, to the nugget and he was taken away in custody by the officers.

Sometime later, Difflo applied for a Writ of Habeas Corpus and, on the pretext of surrendering the nugget; he was allowed to go with two constables to search in Ipswich. He took them on a wild-goose chase around the One Mile Creek and, after pretending to dig at the roots of several trees, he said that he'd forgotten the place where it was buried and was brought back. I expect that his idea was to give the officers 'leg bail' but, finding them armed with a musket, he found that he had miscalculated his chance of escape. Those who hide can find but, as Difflo had never hid, he could not be expected to find.

It is currently reported that his family have the gold, and that they say "He will only stop in gaol for three years and then he will come out, so we keep his nugget quite safe". Other persons besides this stupid and obstinate man, Sir, have suffered loss. I am thirty pounds a loser by the proceedings, having carried on his case on the faith of his honesty. If, therefore, Difflo wants his liberty, don't let him seek it on a false plea. Let him say – 'I am a rogue, but I consider eighteen months sufficient imprisonment for my dishonesty'

I am, Sir,

Your obedient servant, Charles F. Chubb. Ipswich, September, 1861

A reply from the Sheriff's officer:

From The Moreton Bay Courier, Brisbane.

The 7th of September 1861.

The Diffo's Case:

Sir,

In reference to Difflo's case, I can see by Mr Chubb's letter in today's issue, that he says that he was informed by the Sheriff's officer who arrested Difflo, that he saw the nugget on the table in Difflo's house. Now, Mr Editor, I happen to be the officer who arrested Difflo and, in reply to Mr Chubb, I beg to state that I never saw the nugget, neither did I tell Mr Chubb that I saw it, and nor did I tell him that I was directed to arrest only Difflo himself and not the nugget. Neither was Difflo's son present at the time of his father's arrest. I am hoping that you will please insert this in your newspaper.

I am, Sir, Your obedient servant, Charles Davis, Sheriff's Officer.

Charles Difflo's fellow miners were more direct in their support for Difflo's case as the Special Correspondent for the Moreton Bay Courier was to find out when he visited Tooloom and sought their opinions on the gold field itself.

I mean, of course, that very identical nugget that was found by a digger (Difflo), which weighed over eighty oz, and which was delivered over to some person in connection with the Ipswich gold-escort for safety, and in relation to which there was a legal injunction to restrain the digger and finder from taking possession of, until he had been able to justify his alleged ownership in the eyes of the law. My newly found friends pointed out the spot where this large nugget had been found, and told me something in relation to it, which, if I tell the story as nearly as possible as I heard it, I may escape the libel court.

"Ah" said one, "that was a d---shame. That fellow who laid claim to a share of the nugget had no more to do with it than a stranger. He had sold out of the claim the day before, and the finder went early to give the claim a morning trial and found the great nugget. I listened with pleasure. "Lord bless ye," said one, "I never seed a feller in such a way in my life; when he did find it, he didn't know what to do with himself; he turned white and was regularly overcome by it."

"It was his" said another; "and if he'd done as he should, have, he would have kept his find as dark as a chimney sweep." If the party in this claim were jurymen to try the case it would not be difficult to venture a bet of a dozen bottles of champagne on the final outcome of the trial.

Indefinite incarceration for 'Contempt of Court':

Community opinion was sharply divided about the fairness or unfairness of this Supreme Court decision; this was going to keep Charles Difflo in jail until he produced the large Tooloom 80 oz nugget, as the following letters show:

The Courier.

Friday 30th of August 1861.

We have been requested by several intelligent and respectable Germans to draw public attention to the case of one of their countrymen named Difflo, who is at present confined in the Brisbane gaol without much probability of being liberated at any definite date. The man was committed to gaol some eighteen months ago for an offence designated by legal phraseology as 'Contempt of Court'. He has committed an offence that the law recognises and, for that offence, may undergo or at least so it appears, perpetual imprisonment.

The family tragedy continued:

The following letter relates to the evidence taken at an inquest held on Wednesday at the Queensland Hotel, Little Ipswich, on the body of Andow Difflo, a lad of fifteen and son to the Difflo who is in prison for his failure to surrender the 80 oz nugget.

The Moreton Bay Courier

30th of September 1861

From Our Own Correspondent (for Friday 27th of September 1861)

Difflo's daughter Phoebe testified on Friday the 27th of September 1861 at a Coronial inquest into the drowning of her brother - Andow Difflo, in the Three Mile Creek in Ipswich. She told the Coroner that Andow had been leaning over the water when he suffered a sudden fit and had then fallen into the water unconscious and had subsequently drowned.

> *Phoebe's testimony was verified by a local gardener - Gottlieb Franck. He related that he saw an Indigenous person remove the lifeless body of Andow Difflo from the water on that day. The Coroner found that Andow Difflo had died from accidental drowning.*

The tragedy of having no father to support the family, was now compounded by the death of the son. Eventually, after much representation, Governor Bowen released Difflo and Parliament subsequently changed the law regarding sentencing for 'Contempt of Court' so that, in the future, no one could be incarcerated indefinitely.

Difflo was finally freed:

From Pughs Almanac:

> *On the 14th of January 1862, Difflo - a German, who had been incarcerated in Brisbane Gaol for two years and five months for 'Contempt of Court' for not producing a nugget as required in a civil action, was liberated under warrant from the Governor – Sir George Bowen.*

What happen to the nugget? Did he find where it had been buried upon his release? Did his wife recover it and sell it while he was in goal to provide for their family? Was the hiding place lost and never found? All of these questions were pursued in the local newspapers over the following decades, in what became known as the 'Treasure Hunt on Denmark Hill'.

How his family must have suffered whilst he spent nearly two and a half years in gaol, all for a gold nugget worth only £300. This author surmises that he recovered the nugget himself after his release from goal, but we may never know!

The author crevicing for Clarence gold aka sniping
Source: Garry Gatfield, 2024

8

The 'rush' commences

The township of Fairfield (Drake) was the closest local settlement to Tooloom, being situated about 35 miles south of the Tooloom goldfield. It was already established as a base for supplies by the local Diggers and these nearby goldfields were already being worked from 1857 onwards. The discovery of Tooloom, as already mentioned, arose from the prospecting field trips of these established local diggers.

Rumours of new finds were common on all goldfields, including at Tooloom, and often provoked a rush, but not all 'would-be-diggers' were believers.

As one unsourced digger sourly put it:

> *I know of one nugget weighing 15 ounces, but your correspondent - Mr. H. M. (the storekeeper and gold buyer), is well known here and this statement that a nugget of 40 ounces was found is a gross falsehood and, I dare say, an intended misrepresentation, which has been the result of much misery. May I, once for all, warn people generally and those who have a tolerable living especially, not to regard a 'rush' unless such facts are in their hands that there can be no doubt of the reports given.*

We know, however, that the above report by 'H.M.' was correct – a nugget of 41ozs was found at Tooloom in August 1859.

Melancholy Death:

Clarence River

29th of July 1859

Empire, Sydney.

> *The Tooloom correspondent of the Clarence Examiner says:- The diggings at M'Leod's Creek continue to, progress most favourably. Most of the diggers have returned from Tooloom.*
>
> *A melancholy death occurred on the 1st instant, at Mr Smith's Inn, Fairfield. About three weeks ago some persons looking for working bullocks, found a man lying on the ground in the shrub about*

a mile and a quarter from Mr Smith's. He was sick and helpless; he stated that his name was John Brown -a native of Sweden, and that he was travelling with his mate from the Table-land to Tooloom, had camped at that place where he was found and that during the night he was taken very ill, and in the morning was unable to walk; his mate left him, remarking "that if Brown could not walk he would not wait for him." The poor fellow lay there two days and two cold frosty nights before he was discovered. It is a pity that the name is not known, in order that the heartless wretch might be held up to the execration of his follow creatures. The poor follow was conveyed to Fairfield, and Mrs Smith immediately sent for a doctor from Tenterfield, and showed him every possible attention. The diggers in the neighbourhood subscribed £14 for his assistance; still Mrs Smith must be a considerable loser in a pecuniary point of view from his long-continued illness. I understand she has not only paid a heavy doctor's bill, but was also obliged to hire a constant attendant for him. In this case, like too many others, charity must be its own reward.

The same paper gives the following commercial report:

Our various, storekeepers and importers are fast filling up their warehouses in anticipation of an increased trade with the diggings. The news on the whole is favourable, and we doubt not that steady men can make good progress. We desire no rush, and therefore refrain from publishing statements, which may, at a distance, seem impossible. Mr Miller arrived on Sunday from Tooloom, bringing with him, 200 ounces of the precious metal, the result of two days purchasing. Mr Robertson, of Sandilands, has likewise 100 ounces. Mr Miller's account is all that could be desired.

The escort arrived to-day from Timbarra with 1,111 ozs. 3 dwts. 12 grains of gold. The returns would have been much heavier, but for the fact of the Commissioner having recently taken on to Sydney, by way of Armidale and Maitland, 2,600 ozs., which will be set down as gold from that quarter. Henceforth the gold will be forwarded by the Grafton steamer.

John Browns' unfortunate death demonstrates the hardships faced by most diggers in those days, and the need for a reliable and trust-worthy mate. Evidently, the travelling companion of John Brown – was not much of a mate! The rivalry between Grafton and Armidale is also evident from the comment about the gold trade. No longer would the people of Grafton allow *their* gold to be diverted via Armidale, and the Timbarra output to be subsumed into the Uralla Rocky River production figures.

Such false representations:

Original Correspondence, (2nd of August 1859).

To the Editor of the Clarence and Richmond Examiner.

SIR: - In your issue of the 26th of July I observe a paragraph headed "Our Diggings," stating that the Tooloom diggings turned out very unsatisfactorily and that diggers daily returned in forties and fifties to the Timbarra diggings. I believe that your informant must be wrongly informed or acts with personal interest. I have no personal interest in either of those diggings, but merely of curiosity paid a visit to see the various operations of them and cannot omit to contradict such false representations as your correspondent gave.

I was a week at the Tooloom diggings. I visited several parties at work, and saw that merely by scraping with a knife, and washing the stuff in the washing pan, each pan yielded at an average from four to eight pennyweights; in some cases, even more. In that one week I saw more than twenty parties, each party consisting of two or three men, selling at Mr Miller's store from eight to ten ounces per man, and some a larger quantity, for one week's work; other parties four of five ounces each. Mr Robertson bought in one week seven pounds weight, from four parties. If this be unsatisfactory I don't know what is satisfactory, when such a yield is obtained without cradles or proper tools.

I do not say but that some were unsuccessful, as is the case at every diggings. A great number of the diggers possessed from one to three pounds weight, and were unwilling to sell any gold because the price given by the Mint, £3 7s. 11d., was, as the diggers thought, under value. Many parties were prospecting, and found out several good claims, but that a great number of idlers were present on the diggings, thinking that they would get gold by only picking it up, is true also. Some were without means, and of course the store-keepers would not give any more credit to those men who did not choose to work.

There is one gully where those idlers did sink several holes from two to three feet deep, and found actually several specks, in each pan, but did not sink any deeper; 20 holes were dug in this manner and abandoned. In this very same gully now there are at work 15 men, all doing well. Those idlers of course did leave, but only about 20, including those parties who had a claim at the Timbarra diggings, their partners at that place wishing them to return to first work out their claims at Timbarra, with the idea of returning again to the Tooloom.

As to the Geological formation, it is my opinion that the Tooloom diggings will turn out, in a short time, if not the richest in N. S. Wales, a well-paying diggings, only it wants really practical men with means, because it is my positive belief that deep sinking is necessary. You will excuse my taking up so much of your time and space, but I wish the real truth and state of the diggings to be brought before the public.

I remain, Sir, yours &c.,

W. G.

The Pretty Gully Gold Rush:

Clarence and Richmond Examiner and New England Advertiser, (8th of November 1859).

Gold News: Timbarra Diggings

From our Correspondent

During the last fortnight a great many of the miners have been unsettled, through the report of the New Rush at Pretty Gully, near Tabulam. That rush continues to attract, but it is doubtful whether many will remain there during the summer on account of the scarcity of water. The Gold is rough and very similar to the Tooloom metal, but it is Two shillings an ounce more valuable. There is a very good road to it from Tabulam, ten or twelve miles.

2,549 ozs. of Gold:

The Sydney Morning Herald, (1859, November 4).

Grafton

From our Correspondent

The escort arrived yesterday, from Timbarra and Tooloom, bringing the largest amount of gold yet received, viz., 2549 ozs. 13 dwts., and £323 in specie. A sergeant and two troopers have been detached from the Timbarra escort, to convey the treasure from Tooloom and Emu Creek - this was much wanted, as the returns show.

This move has rather checkmated the Ipswichians, notwithstanding the spirit shown by them in starting a private escort to that place; but after all, it is of small importance which road the gold travels by, as Tooloom is only seventy miles from that place, they must ultimately get a large portion of the benefit by supplying the diggers, should the diggings prove permanent, of which there is little doubt at present.

The large nuggets found are causing some excitement; I trust there will be no mad rush in consequence.

Humbug!:

The Moreton Bay Courier, (5th ofNovember 1859).

Tooloom Diggings

(To the Editor of the Clarence and Richmond Examiner.)

Mr Dear Sir, - Not being an apt correspondent, I did not think my initials would again appear at the end of a letter in your enlightened columns, but your excessively pungent and satirical article against Brisbane and Ipswich papers, has urged me to beg of you the insertion of these few lines. I have been residing on different gold-fields in New South Wales a good portion of the time since they were first opened, and, notwithstanding the first unsuccessful trip of the escort (unsuccessful from its unexpected arrival, and from want of confidence, it being only a private escort). I have no hesitation in asserting that, taking into consideration the time the field has been opened, and the small number of diggers we have had on the ground, there has been more gold produced here than on any other diggings in this colony within the same time, including even your favored Fairfield.

The last escort took, within an ounce or two, 480 ounces, and will take considerably more next trip, including a nugget of pure gold found yesterday, weighed by myself, 80 ozs. 17 dwts. 12 grains.

Although similar, this can't be Difflo's Nugget, as this was found in early November.

Instead of abusing this field because loading comes to it from Queensland, try to divert the traffic to your own river. Twenty-five loads of property have been lying months at Lawrence Town, Clarence River, and no teams to bring them up. You accuse the Brisbane and Ipswich papers of humbugging the colonists. Allow me to say, in conclusion, that the greatest piece of humbug I have seen respecting Tooloom is your own article.

I am, Sir, yours, &c., H. M.

Report on all the fields:

The Moreton Bay Courier, (12th of November 1859).

Tenterfield.

From a Correspondent.

I HAVE just completed a ten weeks trip to the different new rushes on and around the Fairfield diggings.

Timbarra, or the Table Land, is now in possession of the Chinese, some 500 in number; the ground having been vacated by Europeans to go to new rushes, they immediately occupied it, and manage to make on an average from £2 to £3 per week per man. Some 6 or 8 claims, the rich ones that were being worked, they have managed to purchase, paying from £40 to £125 for each, so that they have the place almost entirely to themselves - not more than one or two parties of Europeans are left of the hundreds that a short time since filled every creek and gully.

McLeods Creek is also fast following the fate of Timbarra; the water wheels and pumps of its former occupants are now mostly left to the tender mercies of the Celestials. Some of the best claims that were not finished working they bought, and now the whole length and breadth of it is being turned over to great advantage. In some of the large flats that would not pay Europeans, they manage to get first rate wages.

Tooloom is being tried as well as it can. The shortness of water prevents some first-rate ground from being worked to advantage, but it will turn out a much larger quantity of gold soon, as the first rainy season sets in. Even the children of some are earning men's wages, cleaning out crevices. &c. As to size, of gold Tooloom is far ahead of all the Fairfield rushes. Some 15 or 20 nuggets have been turned up, varying from 3 to 16 ozs. each, and one or two much larger.

Nelson's Creek is now being worked with much greater success than when the first rush took place. Several parties are making £1 a day, and claims that yielded only half that amount are the most successful now.

Rocky River is a place that will be steadily opened and finally worked to great advantage. There are great difficulties to contend with that will not suit miners of small means. A great quantity of gold is raised by a very few parties, and kept very silent too.

Maryland Rush is now commencing, but not one party in six is able to make out the whereabouts, and are roaming the country in vain, seeking the mysterious and hidden parties.

There are two or three other creeks nearly finished their first working, and wait quiet until the Chinese commence, when they will again teem with life, and pay them well for years to come.

Stores are coming up from all quarters, and soon it will be as cheap to live well here as in any inland town. Diggers grumble more than over, still the yield of gold increases every month,

I have now to give you a short, but correct account of the present condition of the Fairfield Diggings, and I hope it will not be the means of leading any one astray. Any single man can do well, because he can afford to tramp from one point to another, and if he perseveres is sure before many weeks to meet with a claim to suit him.

Robinson, Nov. 4th, 1859.

Milton working the sluice box
Source: Garry Gatfield, 2024

9

Getting to Tooloom

Journey to Tooloom from the south via Grafton:

The first arrivals of British origin to the Upper Clarence area were convicts escaping from Moreton Bay. These were followed by cedar getters chasing the 'red' gold and the first flocks of the squatters arrived by September 1840:

> *A post office and a store had been established at the head of navigation* (at Copmanhurst) *for the supply of the settlers (Stubbs, 2007: pp. 17-18).*

During 1841, the squatter Ogilvie from Yulgibar set up a dray route from Tenterfield to Grafton; this route descended from Tenterfield to present-day Tabulam before following the Clarence River southward to Copmanhurst. Bales of wool were taken from the drays at Copmanhurst and were then shipped to Grafton (Stubbs, 2007: p.54).

Grafton thus became an important transportation node and was linked by road to the New England Tableland towns of Armidale to the southwest, Glen Innes to the west and Tenterfield to the north-west by 1849 (Stubbs, 2007: pp. 53-54). By 1859, Grafton had already become an ocean-going, regional port on the Clarence River. This river soon became a major route for arriving, would-be gold diggers who were travelling to the new goldfields around the town of Fairfield (later Drake) on the Upper Clarence River (Stubbs, 2007: p. 53-54). The southern route from the inland port of Grafton to the Tooloom Goldfield is shown in the following figure. Note that the course of the Clarence River is not depicted.

This southern route was only about ten miles longer than the Tooloom route from Ipswich via the Fassifern Valley but it was a more difficult route with the Clarence River itself being one of the major obstacles for the arriving diggers at the inland port of Grafton.

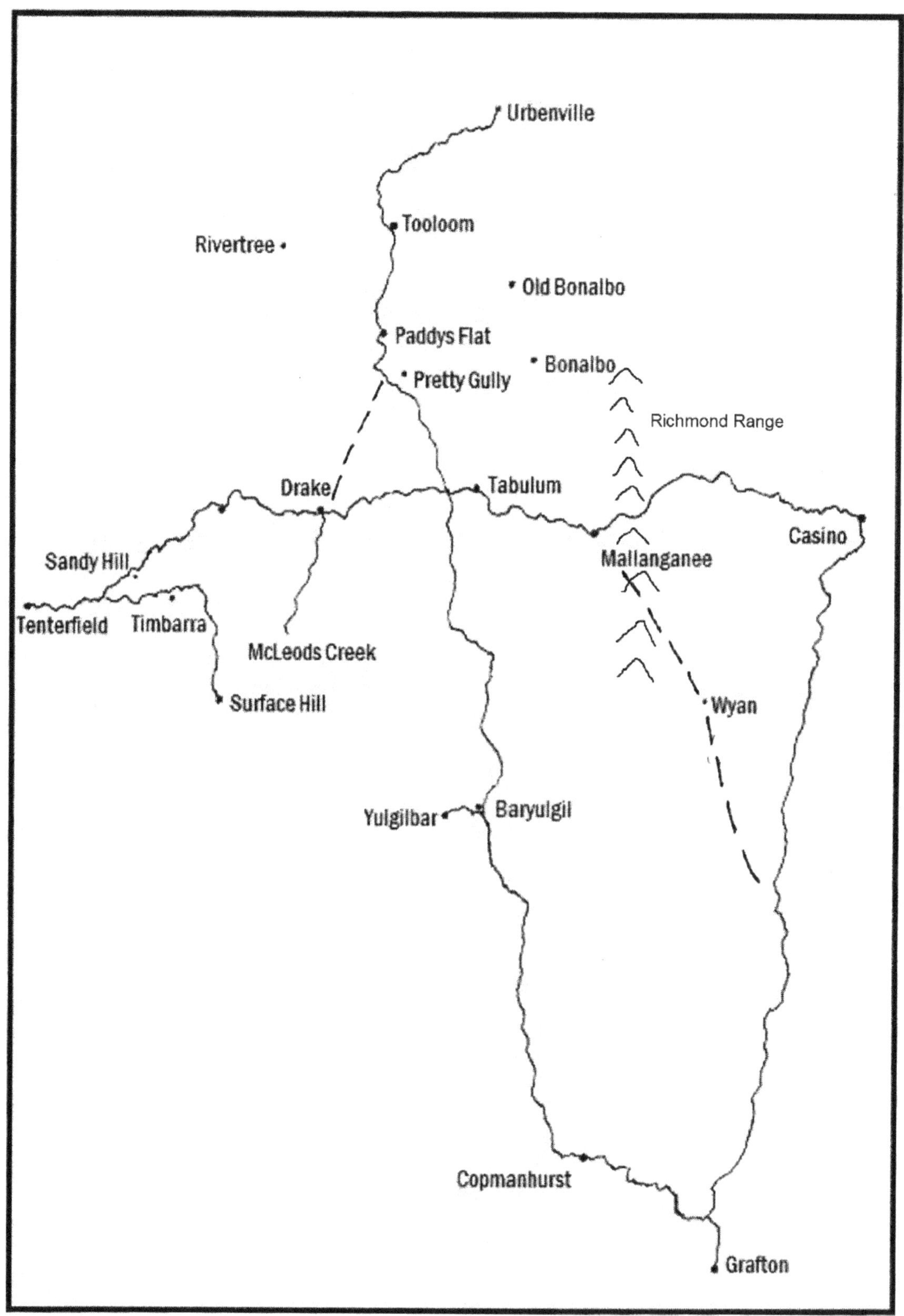

Figure 2. The southern route from Grafton to Tooloom
Source: Garry Gatfield, 2024

There were many difficulties faced by diggers after they disembarked at either Lawrence or Grafton; the journey to Tooloom was an arduous one over rugged terrain. The Richmond Range had to be traversed then there was swamp country, which was followed by the crossing of the mighty Clarence River - one of the 'Big Rivers' of north-eastern New South Wales. The Clarence catchment is approximately 25,000 sq kilometres and is probably home to more snakes than any other district in Australia, which provides an added hazard to the pedestrian! The gold digger had to lose then gain, approximately 1500 ft of elevation to traverse Paddy's Flat and to cross the Clarence again. This was a great disincentive for the bullock drivers with their heavily-laden drays.

A second route was established in 1842. This continued eastwards from Tabulam then crossed the Richmond Range and passed through Busby's Flat and Wyan before reaching the Clarence at Traveller's Rest and, from there, finally reached Grafton (Stubbs, 2007: p55). The 'old road' along the Clarence River was replaced in 1859 by a 'new road', which crossed the Clarence River at Yates Flat before joining the old road to the west of Tabulam on its way to Grafton (Stubbs, 2007).

This 'new road' soon became very popular as one traveller to Tooloom noted in the following letter. This citizen who had forwarded this next account of his journey to Tooloom was simply known as J.S.L. and the following letter gave a description of his journey from Sydney via the southern approach to Tooloom from Grafton. It was published in various papers in late June 1859; examples of such newspapers included *The Maitland Mercury* and *The Hunter River General Advertiser.*

J.S.L's first stop after leaving Sydney on the 'Duncan Hoyle' (captained by Captain Quale) was the new township of Lawrence Town at the Elbow on the Clarence River. This was still a distance of twenty-four miles below the inland port of Grafton. After disembarking, a further half mile took our correspondent to his first night's accommodation at the comfortable Halfway Inn

> *At the Elbow, a wharf and store has been built for the landing of passengers and goods, where they are received and stored by Messrs Stewart, by whom every attention is paid, both to passengers and to merchandise.*

The first stage of the overland journey to the Traveller's Rest entailed a further journey of twelve miles through the squatter's run of C Irving Esq. on an excellent road without any major obstacles before reaching Wyan on the run of Messrs. Fanning and Clarke. These squatters had opened their houses to provide traveller accommodation. Beyond Wyan, there were a number of creeks that needed to be crossed and this was often a daunting task in this region's wet season.

A further journey of another twelve miles over relatively flat country brought the traveller to the Robertson run at the foot of the formidable Richmond Range. This four-mile section was very challenging for both horsemen and drays with two or three severe pinches. After completing the Richmond Range crossing, the traveller had then reached the head of the Big Swamp - a distance of about five miles, and through further runs belonging to Messrs. Robertson of Sandilands (now Mallanganee). There was still thirty-two miles needed from here to reach Tooloom. The latter squatter travelled frequently to Tooloom with his drays and he was thus a font of information for the weary traveller. The distance to Tooloom from the furthest squatting run's outer edge was then a distance of fifteen miles still needed to reach the new Tooloom diggings.

In all, this previous description equated to a total journey of ninety-eight miles from Grafton to Tooloom and consisted of four stages whilst passing through the various grazing runs of the local squatters. These persons were more than willing to provide accommodation and provisions to the passing traveller and, thus, they also benefitted economically from the developing gold rush. This route was certainly less daunting than the earlier described route up the flood-prone Clarence River. J.S.L. - our correspondent, also added an interesting comment about an alternative route to Timbarra via Tabulam:

> *If, however, the traveller wished to reach the Timbarra goldfields, he must pass on to Tabulam where he would have the pleasure of passing over Cowabobbler, close to the beautiful station of Captain Cheval. This was a piece of road, which I think, was almost unequalled in the colony for its jumpers; these were about two to four foot high and required, no doubt, some little care to reach the bottom in safety.*

The traveller had to cross a sandstone escarpment just a few kilometres to the east of Tabulam. It is probable that the jump-ups that were mentioned here related to the sandstone's habit of being layered, so that the dray master had then to negotiate the very steep slopes via a series of steps that varied in height.

> *At this place, Mr Jordan Senior had opened a new accommodation house that had been greatly required in this locality. Tabulam was still ten miles distant from the Big Swamp on the direct road to the Fairfield diggings.*
>
> *From Tabulam to the Clarence Inn at Fairfield is fifteen miles. About one mile from the former place, you will have to ford the river. This, at the head of the Clarence is easily accomplished when the weather is favourable, but it is extremely dangerous in a flood when the water will rise 12 to 20 feet in a few days. The Clarence Inn in Fairfield is the property of Mr George Smith who has just completed the new house in the very best style and with every convenience that can possibly be required.*
>
> *Opposite this inn is a road to the diggings at Tooloom, but this is longer and not as good as the former. About two miles from there is also a road to the Table Land diggings at Timbarra, which is fifteen miles from Fairfield - and is such a road that surely a fox hunter in merry England never encountered. It took us four hours with capital horses to bring us to the end of fifteen miles.*
>
> *J.S.L.*

Journey to Tooloom from Moreton Bay

The route taken by the *Moreton Bay Courier's 'Special Correspondent'* to the Tooloom goldfields in 1859 from Brisbane and Ipswich, went down the Fassifern Valley and crossed over what is now the Queensland - New South Wales Border. This route was just over 100 miles (160km) from Brisbane and the distance from Ipswich was shorter by 20 miles. Tooloom goldfield thus lay within a reasonable travelling distance from the main population-centres of Queensland's Moreton Bay Settlement (later Brisbane) and Ipswich. The distance from Tooloom to the coastal port of

Grafton was a similar distance as the Ipswich route but those southern diggers had to face greater difficulties along their way.

Today, the most direct route from Brisbane is via Beaudesert and, from the latter, this route then follows the Mt Lindsey Highway through Rathdowney to Woodenbong and from there, makes a southern turn-off to Urbenville before finally continuing on to Tooloom Creek.

During my research in the Trove Archives, I was very fortunate to discover the nine letters that had been written towards the end of 1859 by the anonymous *'Special Correspondent'* for the *Moreton Bay Courier*. They provided a unique viewpoint of life in a 'gold rush' in those roaring days. Selected edited excerpts from these letters are used herein to illustrate the *'Special Correspondent's'* description of life on the Tooloom goldfield and in the township of Tooloom and of the difficulties that the miners faced in the 'gold rush' of 1859.

The *'Special Correspondent'* had arrived in Moreton Bay following the recent Canoona gold rush of 1858 This had ended badly and the northern colony's reputation had suffered for many years.

In his first letter on the 26th of November 1859, the *'Special Correspondent'* recorded his first impressions of the likely success of the Tooloom goldfield as gleaned from passers-by returning from Tooloom. On his journey via Woogaroo (Goodna), he had met and questioned a certain Mr Holmes who was travelling with his son; these two had previously walked to Tooloom in four days. After his enquiry about where he had come from, Homes had responded:

> *From Tooloom, said he. What news, friend? said I. Bloody bad, said Holmes, I toiled a long, long time, and though I found the colour, I could find no more.*

Holmes, his son and friend had just spent four weeks on the Tooloom diggings and his opinion was that one needed fifty or sixty pounds just to be able to hang on. His main complaint was that the best claims were already taken, and he thought that newcomers had no prospect of success unless new payable claims were found. This was a major complaint from many miners on the goldfields of Eastern Australia in the 1850s and beyond.

The opinion of Holmes about Tooloom was reinforced by the reply of one 'John' to whom the *Special Correspondent* had later addressed a similar enquiry:

> *I have had my share of experience since I left Brisbane; and it's my opinion the diggings are no good,* said John, then adding somewhat ominously:
>
> *From the accommodation house at the foot of the range to Tooloom will give you a teasing!*

Despite this discouragement, our *'Special Correspondent'* took time out to admire the splendid new road that had been built to Ipswich from Brisbane:

> *I trust Tooloom will not turn out to be 'a shicer.' If it does, allow me to congratulate the inhabitants of Brisbane and Ipswich on the splendid road, which is opening up between the towns.*

He would later be less sure about the road upon leaving Balbi's Inn, saying then:

> *To describe the roadway for horses and foot travellers here would not increase the desire that might animate the settlers in towns to try their fortune at the diggings.*

Figure 3. The northern journey to Tooloom from Brisbane
Source: Garry Gatfield, 2024

Travelling from Ipswich to Fassifern:

> *Saddled and off again. A sharp canter of a mile brought the traveller into a beautiful open country with thinly timbered grass looking greener than in the neighbourhood of Brisbane and the country partaking of that character gave one a realization of profitable pastoral occupation. The country was almost as splendid as a gentleman's park ...*

On the 30th of November 1859, the '*Special Correspondent*' reached the 'murdering hut' eleven miles from Ipswich where the gentle undulations and fine appearance of the wide-opened spaces in the countryside prompted him to consider that country like this could provide a solution for England's poverty woes. Whilst realising that this hut marked a place where there had been a massacre of white pastoralists, the '*Special Correspondent*' noted that the indigenous warriors behind this massacre here might well have been motivated by their indignation about being dispossessed from such a well-favoured place. This was a very perceptive comment for 1859.

The '*Special Correspondent*' had by now reached the 'Fifteenth Mile Water Hole' where the Peak Mountain (Flinder's Peak) dominated the landscape.

Our 'Special Correspondent' also had no doubt about the utility of this route to the Tooloom goldfields:

> *The road was alive with traffic. I saw no fewer than twenty-one drays and had an opportunity of yarning with a good-natured lot of bullock-drivers ... The difficulties and dangers of the way from Ipswich to Balbi's are not to be mentioned. The whole distance was a well-beaten road.*
>
> *This day's journey done finds me comfortably located at Balbi's ... Mr Balbi, as an innkeeper, evidently understands his calling - no greater praise need be given by your correspondent.*

Our '*Special Correspondent*' also learnt at Balbi's that:

> *The (gold) escort was expected here tonight returning from Tooloom.*
>
> And that:
>
> *For the past fortnight, while prospecting between Balbi's and Cunningham's Gap. Miners had obtained 'the colour' in most places and that there are hopes entertained that a gold field will soon be found within fifteen miles of Fassifern.* (Note: It wasn't found!).

TOOLOOM DIGGINGS.

The nearest and best road to Tooloom Diggings from Brisbane and Ipswich is by way of the BUSH INN, FASSIFERN.

Alexander Balbi

PROPRIETOR of the Bush Inn, Fassifern, respectfully informs all travellers in Queensland that they can be supplied with first-class accommodation at his hotel.

A good SPREAD is provided daily.

The Beds are first-class and the comforts at the Bush Inn, Fassifern, will bear honorable comparison with any first-class house in the colony.

Good Stabling and Paddock for Horses. The Paddock is free of charge and is well grassed and watered. Fassifern is an easy day's stage from Ipswich, and also an easy distance from the Accommodation House at the foot of the Range.

Parties are informed that the IPSWICH ESCORT calls at the Bush Inn; and Merchants, Gold-buyers and Diggers requiring directions from Fassifern to Tooloom should call at the Bush Inn, the proprietor having marked a new line of road which saves a distance of some miles.

Balbi's Bush Inn Advertisement

Source: via Trove

The above advertisement promoted the comforts of Balbi's Inn to the weary traveller such as our '*Special Correspondent*'. It would have looked very enticing to the weary digger or to an exhausted reporter such as himself.

Travelling from Fassifern to the Kooreelah Range:

The way to Tooloom then became more challenging as described by the '*Special Correspondent*'. After he had departed Balbi's Bush Inn on the morning of the 6th of December 1859; he made the following observations, perhaps he had spoken about the quality of the road too soon!

> *My last (letter) left you advised of my arrival at Balbi's and, of my intention to fetch up with some intending Tooloomers, who were leaving the 'Bush Inn' in Fassifern, when I arrived.*
>
> *On Wednesday morning, I made an early start and, soon after, I was on the track for the noted scrub through which travellers have to pass.*
>
> *Under the shade of mountains, beautiful in appearance and majestic in height and boldness, the track wound circuitously until a creek was reached, at which point skirting the water, the way was then made into the scrub, which was about one mile and a-half through ...*
>
> *The reader may picture a stone staircase, which was very irregularly laid by the hands of Dame Nature and ornamented with overhanging trees, from which the traveller on horseback must be extremely careful to protect his cranium. A horse is also required to be sure-footed and well-bottomed and, if possessing both these qualifications, the journey may be made with an occasional slip ... At the top of the hill and at the end of the scrub, a slip rail had to be passed into Messrs. Hardy and Weinholt's Paddock, which by the way, was of considerable size and as large as a comfortable estate and, after descending from no mean elevation, the way was good to Moograh.*
>
> *Moograh,* (Moogerah an out-station belonging to Fassifern) *was delightfully situated on the top of a gently, rising knoll; it had a small lagoon at its front and was sheltered by mountains on all sides save for the road on which I was to travel. I was interested to discover that Moograh comes from an aboriginal word 'Moojirah' meaning home of the thunderstorm.*
>
> *Near to this point, however, the dray road joined the foot path and I, having reached the point where I might with safety pursue my way alone, my guide received my thanks for his kindness and returned to Balbi's.*
>
> *After descending a sharp hill, I came up with a bullock-dray laden with goods belonging to Mr Fleming, who also happened at that time to come up on his road from Tooloom. He acquainted me with the fact that the escort was 'close up', and that some six hundred ounces of gold was in their possession. I learned afterwards that two men who were in Mr Fleming's company also had some three hundred ounces in their possession, of which they were the bona fide owners and finders.*

From the Fourteen Mile Station to 'The Accommodation House' at the foot of the Kooreelah Range was about eight miles. The way was not first-class, but the road was so well beaten that a stranger could not miss it.

Wednesday night brought me then, to the foot of the Kooreelah Range and, not being disposed to try the journey further that night, I made up my mind to camp with Pat Carney who had erected a large shanty, whence he dispensed board and lodging, and gave information of the grounds of Beulah to the tired and footsore wayfarers.

Pat Carney, aka Barney Carney, after whom Barney Point on the Tweed River was named, was a man of mystery; he had other aliases besides. Some suspect he may have been trying to hide possible convict ancestry, but he was recognised as a good 'mine host' to the weary diggers on their travels to and from Tooloom.

Traversing the Kooreelah Range after leaving Carney's:

Up! Up! Up! For three or four miles, until 'Vinegar Hill' was neared. At this pinch, what with loose stones and the steepness of the ascent, the place had better have been named 'The Mount of Difficulty' Up and down - now slipping, another time scrambling, all the while being careful to make headway with perspiration oozing from every pore and with the horse groaning and rushing until the top was climbed. Then there was a sight worth looking at!

Mountain seemed piled upon mountain; in the distance beneath lay range after range - the line of mountains near to Balbi's now looked small and Switzerland could not have boasted of finer mountain scenery.

Our '*Special Correspondent*' didn't inform us of the name of this mountain that this ascent occurred upon, but this editor speculates, from the way that the track here crossed what is now called 'The Border Range' between Mts Ballow and Clunie, that Mt Clunie was indicated. Mt Clunie is one of the higher mountains (1158 m) on the Queensland - New South Wales State border.

All travellers over the first Kooreelah Range from Carney's Accommodation House were told that for the first nine miles of the way, there was no water and, if they were wise, they would provide themselves with some - as the difficulty of carriage would be amply repaid by the pleasure of a drink.

It should be noted now, that a National Park covers the headwaters of Koreelah Creek on the southern side of the Scenic Rim, in northern New South Wales.

This day (Thursday), the '*Special Correspondent*' made about thirty miles to the foot of the Tooloom Range, at which place he camped under a bullock dray and heard the yarning of six returning diggers and, in the morning at an early hour, he then made haste to Tooloom.

A final challenge before reaching Tooloom:

After reaching the slip-rail of Tooloom cattle station or paddock, an easy distance from this brought me to a splendid waterfall called Tooloom Falls.

The reader must picture some fifty or sixty feet of rock roadway on one side of which was a deep-water level with the rocks, and on the other side, a depth of thirty feet with that part nearest the falls being in the shape of an arc. The passage over these rocks was extremely dangerous. The action of the water had worn deep chasms and holes in the roadway; this was not at all favourable to the wheels of bullock drays or to the legs of horses and men. That part of the rock roadway nearest to Tooloom was not more than fifteen or sixteen feet in width and it required all the care of the drivers to make a sure passage. The usual mode of transit was to fasten on a double team of bullocks, so that those in front would keep the line straight and, thus, drag over the other drays.

When the water rushed over the falls with great rapidity, foot passengers usually had to resort to a log of timber to secure themselves whilst passing the most dangerous part. Judging from the appearance of the place in dry weather and what dangers the not very pleasant passage afforded at such times when only a small quantity of water was running, I cannot say that I would have felt any great inclination to risk my neck on so perilous a passage as it must be in the wet season, even though Tooloom nuggets were found to be plentiful on the opposite shore.

Milton 'viewing' for gold on a Clarence River goldfield aka 'sniping'
Source: Garry Gatfield, 2024

10

Tooloom Township

Most mining townships on the eastern Australian goldfields in the 1850s had a sameness about them; this advertised their temporary nature to any traveller passing through them. Housing was very basic, and huts and shelters could thus be easily abandoned when the miners got wind of a new strike elsewhere and these then rushed off to stake new claims in areas of supposed 'big nugget' finds.

There were multiple examples of various types of general store outlets and accommodation providers, but Tooloom was typical of such mining towns at the time in that it lacked many higher-order functions. There were no health practitioners, schools or churches. This then limited the town to having a predominance of single males; the families of the diggers would have found it difficult to accompany their men folk here, although some diggers did have their older sons with them. What tradespeople were in Tooloom were there to service the immediate needs of the miners; two such examples were the town's blacksmith and baker. We do have an eye-witness report again on the state of Tooloom township from our *Moreton Bay Courier's 'Special Correspondent'* in late 1859.

On to Tooloom via Sugar Loaf Mountain:

> *After passing the spectacular Sugar Loaf Mountain with its well-prospected lower sides, a level road of two or three miles then brought the traveller alongside the gullies leading to Tooloom Creek. From 'The Falls' to Tooloom is called the 'twelve mile' and a long and weary twelve miles it is - but what of that when the diggings are so near!*

This above concludes the first part of our 'Special Correspondent's' journey from Ipswich to Tooloom Diggings. This approach from the northern side was on what was then called Carney's Creek Road, out of Boonah. The reader will note that this writer had specifically mentioned that he *'had made up his mind to camp with Pat Carney, who had erected a large shanty to provide board and lodgings to the weary traveller'.* This route then followed the pre-existing Aboriginal track across what is now known as the Border Ranges.

Arrival in Tooloom: The general stores and the blacksmiths:

A banner was flying from the store of Mr. Miller upon which was written words to guide those who needed information about where to purchase goods; 'Tooloom Stores' in large letters kept the friends of the storekeeper from going astray.

Mr Betts figured as a general storekeeper and a little way above him was Mr Gordon who was also a general storekeeper; opposite was a large calico building (about to be supplanted by a slab one), which was said to belong to Mr Fleming. Messrs. Black and Co kept a store near the creek. The ring of the blacksmith's anvil sounded close at hand and, from between the sheets of bark came sparks of fire, which were not sufficiently powerful enough to indulge the fancy that Vulcan was forging thunderbolts. The abode of the 'Vulcan of Tooloom' had belonged to an Ipswich man a few days before my arrival but he had sold out to a German - Mynheer Something. This man was labouring away with all the ardour of a new tradesman when I passed.

The public houses:

Mr Brooks had rigged up a place called 'The Prospector's Arms' and a painting had been employed to aid the calligraphic art, for there now shone the pick and shovel on his signboard; these are emblems of the digging trade, under the shade of which the workers may take their grog and discourse upon the precious metal and upon their chances of finding it. Mr Black had, however, preserved the aboriginal dialect and his house rejoiced under the appellation of 'The Tubra'. This last place formed the headquarters of your correspondent, who, as a kind of cosmopolitan in his own way, wished all parties well with bundles of fun and piles of gold. I must not say how many private grog shops were on the Tooloom diggings, but I have no doubt that every accommodation house that had a sheet of bark for a bedstead and blankets for sheets, with counter-panes and all, could muster their little kegs and drops of various kinds of creature comforts, which helped to keep up the spirits and, which are, often times, productive of little scenes not fit for modest eyes or to be heard by ears polite. I close my brief sketch of the hotels by hoping that all at Tooloom may find it to be other than just 'a land of promise'."

Night in Tooloom:

I heard Mr Fleming praised for the prompt and liberal supply of flour, which he sent. 'We were nearly starved," said a digger to me, "I had nearly a month on beef and peas, and if I had been required to have held out much longer, it would have cooked my goose."

Well! My companion at the hotel is a grazier. He has brought about 1000 sheep so that the diggers might be supplied with mutton. He evidently looks upon me with distrust, which a political yarn did not lessen. The squatter could not convince me and I could not convert him, so off we went to bed in the same room, though on different shake downs; he believed in my rascality, and I believed in his cool impudence - two delightful companions to be closeted together for a night. I admired many notions that he entertained and I liked what squatterdom had done for him; it had made him dare to assert his beliefs. Ownership of flocks and herds are powerful incentives for making a man independent in his feelings. Well - A good night to you all and may my friend understand me better in the morning!"

We are now in Tooloom; a rough and ready city of bark huts, canvass tents and calico-roofed shanties. Board and lodging and accommodation are also signified at various places here.

Dave Smith's Mining Camp at Tooloom 1980
Source: Garry Gatfield, 2024

This photo above depicts the camp of Mr Dave Smith as it was in June 1980. He was the last remaining gold prospector still residing on the Tooloom goldfield. Mr Smith's home consisted of a corrugated iron roof and walls that enclosed a calico tent. Near here, the author obtained his first small nugget - a half pennyweight (0.8g) piece, which he found upstream from this place in a small side gully.

Mr Smith regarded his home as being quite typical of previous diggers' homes in the Tooloom township from the 'gold rush' era. (Smith, D. Pers. Comm. 1980).

Our *Special Correspondent's* first impression upon arriving at the outskirts of Tooloom was of the awful smell emanating from the slaughter yard. Any lingering hostility that the established squattocracy may have had towards this influx of miners into their pastoral leases, soon gave way to an appreciation of these same miners as a new market for their beef and mutton. Without this reliable supply of fresh meat, the miners would have starved, but they still hungered for non-mouldy flour to make their own bread or damper.

The Moreton Bay Courier

8th of December 1859

From our Special Correspondent

As a man travels, he should keep his eyes open, so pardon me for a few moments if I linger to describe Tooloom. I saw the aristocracy of the place in the distance. The Gold Commissioner -

Mr Master, was sunning himself in front of his office-parlour and was holding a morning confab with the Sergeant of the gold police who, as he nodded approvingly to what the King of Tooloom had said, shook the veil with which he had garlanded his hat and beat his long boots with a switch. By the side of these representatives of the law and gospel of Tooloom, stood the oldest storekeeper - Mr Miller; the trio were evidently discussing the probabilities of the new arrival at such a strange hour and in such questionable shape as myself.

Whatever the townships of other diggings may have been when in their infancy, Tooloom reminded me most of a village fair. The wares of the storekeepers were exposed to view in tempting forms and there was an attempt to imitate the shop-keeping, or, more properly, the stall-keeping, of a gala day in a village. The flies were busy with the remaining stock-in-trade of the butcher, whose shop-block looked as if it was 'first chop' for the purpose for which it was intended. The chimney of the baker's oven, which was constructed of corrugated iron, roared its head in pride above the calico roofing; all inside the establishment looked as clean and neat as a penny twist.

The Bridge on Tooloom Creek 2023
Source: Garry Gatfield, 2024

11

Tooloom Goldfield 1859 to 2024

The Tooloom goldfield was always destined to only be an alluvial goldfield until large mining equipment could be carried into this area at a reasonable cost. Mr Fleming's bullock drays of 1859 did not fit into this category. It was a very slow and expensive mode of transport in those years. The miners also faced other major difficulties such as a seasonal lack of water and a lack of new ground that could be made available to the new-comers. The most favoured claims were located in a number of gold-rich gullies that fed into Tooloom Creek and along the bed and banks of the creek itself. These claims were all taken early on in the rush and had been intensively worked - several times over, in some cases.

Difficulties for the miners at Tooloom:

The lack of permanent water at Tooloom in the seasonal gullies away from the main stream, certainly compounded the problem of mining hilly areas distant from Tooloom Creek, as the *'Special Correspondent'* explained in his letters of his journey to Tooloom in late 1859 as follows:

> *The hilly character of the country prevents many patches of good payable ground being worked; there being no water in the ranges to prospect with gold existing in many places on the surface and dams have been constructed to hold the rainwater when it falls. A party of Germans had pack horses for a short time and brought the washing stuff to the river; shooting it down bark shoots 100 foot to the water below. The process was, however, too slow and too expensive and so was soon abandoned.*

While water was in short supply, it did help, if transport was available to carry the wash dirt to a suitable dump point, so the alluvial wash could be processed by sluice box or cradle after rain. The ever-hopeful digger scanned the screens for any nuggets before the tailings were disposed of but the rock strata of the Emu Creek Formation at Tooloom also contained much fine gold derived from the stockworks (swarms of small veins), from thin quartz lodes and from quartz reefs; the lucky miner found plenty of those during the gold rush days. These hard-rock areas, however, required expensive mining tools and equipment for extraction and crushing, so were mostly beyond the scope of the early alluvial miner. Another difficulty faced was that there was an urgent need for better tools and for sawn timber to make sluice boxes, cradles and dwellings at Tooloom in the early days.

From *The Clarence and Richmond Examiner*

28th of June, 1859.

> *There are no sluice boxes used. The miners are working in the dry gullies, with small water-holes where they turn out gold. There is nothing used but the dish, there being nothing else to make cradles.*

Mining with just a dish, pick and shovel was thus the general rule at Tooloom in 1859.

A common complaint from the diggers:

The patchy nature of the gold found at Tooloom was also a very common complaint in 1859; all the best areas had been taken up quickly by the first comers, whilst late arrivals could not find more than just 'a bit of colour' away from the golden gullies. Given the lack of good tools on this difficult-to-access goldfield, the easy- to-work, alluvial creeks, gullies and creek flats were the highly desirable digging locations, and these were intensively prospected and claimed. The best alluvial areas were, however, soon worked out.

From: *The Moreton Bay Courier*

By The 'Special Correspondent'

27th of December, 1859.

> *Under present circumstances, the difficulty is to find new claims; and this I found to be the cause for so many returning. Above all things, a digger who goes to Tooloom should be provided with some 'tin,' that he may hold out.*

Even on the richest alluvial grounds of Tooloom, some gold miners were more fortunate than others. The best alluvial areas were in those creeks and gullies that were adjacent to Triassic igneous intrusions in the sparsely exposed areas of the Palaeozoic Emu Creek Formation. Joe's Gully is one famous gully in that regard. It has produced a copious amount of nuggety alluvial gold, with the premier slug being the 140 oz Lady Bowen Nugget, but it also produced at least one famous specimen of rare cubic crystal gold. There were other rich payable gullies at Tooloom such as Fay's Gully, Dry Gully, Doctor's Gully, Peg Leg Gully and the Eight-Mile or Lower Tooloom.

Gradually some mechanical mining aids did become available. Quartz crushing became popular in the 1870s with storekeepers' records of this time suggesting that just over 874 ounces of gold had been won from crushed quartz in the Tooloom, Pretty Gully and Lunatic Reef area in 1877. The discovery of John Payne's 'Rise and Shine' reef in 1891 saw a new but brief spike of interest in hard rock gold mining at Tooloom but most mining in the 1890s was still only focused on the mining of alluvial ground (*The Warwick and Times Examiner*, 1861-1919).

Fresh food was scarce in the early days of the rush:

Food was very expensive at Tooloom even after Mr Fleming and the Ipswich storekeepers had come to the miners' rescue by sending up dray-loads of flour and other staples. The squatters had enthusiastically embraced the opening of this new market for their flocks; beef and mutton were plentiful and Tooloom had its own butcher with a slaughter yard, but there was a general shortage of other foods at a reasonable price. Note: Slaughteryard Gully is marked on the Tooloom Creek Gold Field Map and is located just north of the main township site.

Fresh vegetables were more difficult to come by for these required a long journey by bullock dray during which, fresh vegetables often had acquired a wilted state on their arrival. It wasn't until later when the Chinese diggers arrived and established their usual market gardens, that the average digger could obtain fresh vegetables reliably and at a reasonable price.

The *'Special Correspondent'* from the *Moreton Bay Courier* quoted one miner as saying:

> *Stores of all kinds are plentiful and cheap, thanks to the enterprise of Queensland, the inhabitants of which seem determined that the diggers shall never want again, gold or no gold. Just now, vegetables would be a blessing indeed. Potatoes, onions, pumpkins, etc, would sell well, and prove a seasonable change from the eternal damper and salt beef.*

The lack of coinage provided a further difficulty:

Coins to pay for the miners' gold were also in short supply and this led to petitions to the Royal Mint in England for the establishment of a branch of the Royal Mint in Sydney. Melbourne was outraged by an agreement that saw a new Mint set up in Sydney in 1855; Melbourne rightly regarded itself as the premier gold producer in the Australian Colonies at that stage. Melbourne eventually got its own Mint in June 1872. Ten tons of copper tokens had to be collected and removed from circulation before the currency could be stabilised around the use of an Australian sovereign and half-sovereign, which had prior approval of the Royal Mint in London.

Coarse alluvial gold from the Clarence River, typical of Tooloom

Source: Garry Gatfield, 2024

The gold in the previous picture is typical of the gold that was found on the Tooloom goldfields, with nuggets up to 1 troy oz. but with many smaller pieces of coarse gold. This gold was panned and sluiced by this author with the help of his cousin - Milton. It is not very often that a fossicker can pan or snipe a 1oz nugget these days, but Milton and I have achieved that on a number of occasions in our prospecting careers!

Nuggety ground at Tooloom:

The Sydney Morning Herald

22nd of October, 1859.

The Correspondent from the Clarence Examiner, writing from these diggings to this journal, said:

> *The Tooloom diggings extend over about thirty miles and pay good wages generally but that is all. A few parties here as on all gold-fields are, of course, more fortunate than the rest but many of the more adventurous gold-seekers get nothing at all.*
>
> *Nuggets from one to three ounces are frequently discovered; in fact, two of the leads consist only of nuggety ground.*
>
> *The claims on the main lead (at Tooloom) are the best, with all the parties doing well. In Big Joe's Gully, two or three patches have paid the lucky finders for lots of duffers' that they had become used to during the preceding weeks.*

Professor Liversidge:

In 1887, the informative work on the occurrences of gold and other mineral resources in New South Wales by Professor Archibald Liversidge, was published. It provided a list of large nuggets found by weight of gold in that colony. He listed the Lady Bowen Nugget from the Tooloom goldfields in 1860 (sic.) as 10th on his list with a weight of 11lbs 8 oz or 140 oz; this large nugget find was not an isolated case as the Tooloom nugget list earlier shows.

The Cubic Crystal Gold Specimen from Joe's Gully:

The following mineral specimen of rare crystalline gold had been found by a miner in Joe's Gully, and later acquired by the noted mineralogist - George Smith; he was an Inspector of Mines in NSW and, consequently, had the opportunity to become a keen collector. This specimen was the largest of several pieces found in Joe's Gully during the late 1800's, and apparently modern day machinery miners have also recovered some additional specimens, but I digress! In George Smith's own words:

> *The most perfect crystallisations were found at Joe's Gully, near Tooloom in a small seam of crushed Andesite, the gold occurring in the rock at the junction of two joints. Only 3ozs. were*

obtained, but all were beautifully crystallised. One group comprised several inter-crystallised cubes, the largest of which was slightly under half an inch across its largest diameter. All the cubes showed hollow faces with sharp angles and edges.

After his retirement, c1927, George Smith sold or donated a large part of his personal collection to the Sydney Museum. It disappeared from the collection of the Mineral Museum in Sydney around 1948 under mysterious circumstances. It was handled by a number of collectors and mineral dealers in Australia, before it headed overseas. It was in the USA until relatively recently, but it has since been sold for an extremely high price and now resides in a private collection in Lebanon. Joe's Gully also produced over 1 ton of gold and most of the bigger nuggets including the 'Lady Bowen Nugget' and the 'Difflo Nugget' but perhaps its crystalline gold is its most rare and treasured bounty!

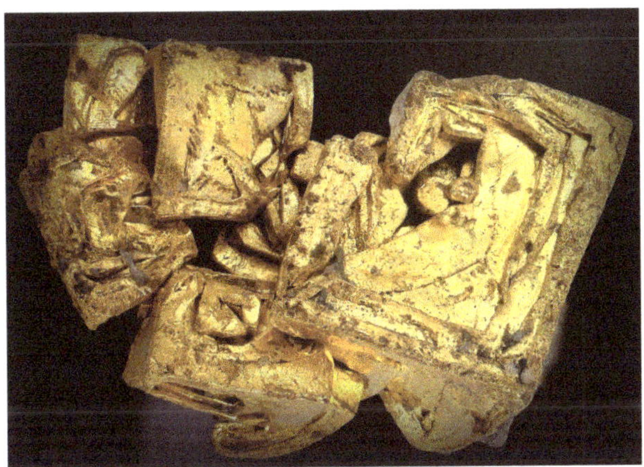

The missing Gold Crystal Specimen from Joe's Gully at Tooloom

Source: Unknown, modified by Garry Gatfield, 2024

The Special Correspondent for the Moreton Bay Courier had ventured down to Joe's Gully to write a report on gold mining therein on the morning after his arrival at Tooloom. His report follows:

The appearance of the bed of Joe's Gully has been entirely altered by the diggers. The bed of the gully is not very wide, but stupendous banks protect it on each side near to the bed of the creek and, here, the busiest operations are being carried on.

At the time of the *'Special Correspondents'* visit in mid-December 1859, there was especially vigorous activity taking place on one large claim, where the team was being led by an Austrian whose party was reputed to have taken out of the claim:

Five pounds weight of gold a day or two before the 'Special correspondent' had reached there.

The *'Special Correspondent'* reported on the unusual type of every-day endeavours that were being undertaken in Tooloom Creek below him:

The Austrian then was very busy on the morning in question. The rough crane was lustily plied to pile huge boulders on one side of the claim, and, over a portion of the sinking, the water appeared; that is the water from the sinking, one of nature's under currents, or cellars, where she, like a good house-wife, keeps a supply of water against a time of need. The bowline cry of the sailor rose as altogether the party hauled and boulder after boulder was elevated to the pile. The Austrian's authority seemed recognised; he had the reputation of being what is known as 'a lucky dog' - whatever he did, turned out right. Such was the general opinion on the field.

Apparently, the Austrian did know what he was doing. Joe's Gully adjoining Tooloom Creek had another unique characteristic that determined how the gold would be found in this famous location.

This author and his cousin Milton did a little bit of exploring in the Tooloom goldfield in the 1980s and early 1990s and talked to a number of small miners in Joe's Gully and in the Lower Tooloom area. Some of these were engaged in machinery mining of the still remaining payable alluvium. Garry and Milton heard of how the gold supposedly occurred in Joe's Gully from a contemporary article by a Cairn's consultant mining engineer; their discussions with the current miners and their own observations in the Joe's Gully area then allowed them to verify his reported information about Joe's Gully for themselves.

These Joe's Gully alluvials are situated in a V-shaped, difficult-to-access gully and it has been hand-mined and re-mined extensively since its initial discovery by the Californian miner – Big Joe, in mid-1859. The Cairns mining engineer believed that this gully had never been comprehensively worked because of its location and because of how the gold occurred in it.

The most favoured area for mining at the Joe's Gully site in 1859 was near the mouth of the gully where it joined with Tooloom Creek. This report had also noted that the gold specifically occurred in the bed of the gully in a thin green-clay layer on top of the bedrock. To mine this required the removal of large boulders from the bedrock in the gully; some of these boulders had weighed several tons.

The Cairns mining consultant's report had also estimated that only about 15% of the Joe's Gully area had been effectively mined whilst 85% of the clay below the big intersecting boulders in the bed of the gully was anticipated to still lie untouched.

The sedimentary rocks of the Tooloom goldfield consist of mainly gently-folded conglomerates, sandstones, carbonaceous siltstones and tuffs of the Emu Creek Formation. These rocks are now thought to have been of Devonian-Carboniferous age and to have been a rifted extension of the Tamworth Belt's forearc basin. The 'golden gullies' had all been heavily worked for alluvial gold during the 1859 to 1862 gold rush and many large nuggets had been found in these gullies; this area had, however, only been minimally worked for hard rock gold by way of digging shafts. There are still a few scattered shafts around Tooloom's hillsides today and these were all mainly emplaced after 1862 (McKay and Wake, 2015).

After 1999, mapping carried out by exploratory gold company - Malachite Resources NL, identified four intrusive bodies in these gullies. These finds were located at Joe's Gully, at Fraser's and at Cullen's Gully in the Tooloom goldfield area and a fourth find was located in 2007 some distance to the north at Phoenix. The Malachite Resources geologists recognised these as being similar to the rare Intrusion-Related Gold-Deposit Systems or IRGDs, which had recently been found and described in Alaska's and in the Yukon's Tintina goldfield (McKay and Wake, 2015).

These IRGDs are known to be associated with orogenic gold.

Dennis and Garry inspecting a shaft at Slaughteryard Gully in 1980
Source: Garry Gatfield, 2024

This small shaft is located near Saughteryard Gully and is upstream from the crossing to the old township site on Tooloom Creek at Billy May's Point. This photo was obviously posed, as no-one would ever actually detect over a shaft like that.

Gold mineralisation at Tooloom is clearly associated with these major intrusion centres. Each of the first three gullies - Joe's, Fraser's and Cullen's are associated with a number of significant gold occurrences, that are both within and adjacent to the intrusion complexes. At Joe's Gully and at Cullen's and Fraser's intrusive centres, the gold resides in narrow, sheeted quartz veins and within stockworks within the Emu Creek Formation's sedimentary rocks. These are usually adjacent to felsic dolerite dykes. Visible gold can also be seen in outcropping quartz veins that surround the Frasers intrusive centre, with gold values up to 100 g/t. Nuggets of varying size can also be found in the creeks and gullies of these area as previously described by (Mckay and Wake, 2015).

Other sources of gold at Tooloom:

Not all of the alluvial gold came, however, from the intrusives quartz veins at Tooloom in the days of the gold rush; a significant part of it had been locally eroded out of older placer deposits that had been buried beneath a Late Permian to Triassic igneous cap that was reputed to have been formed over this area by the Tweed volcano over 23 million years ago. This author and his contributing editor consider that this heavily weather basalt is more like to be of an older Permian to Triassic age.

About 23 million years ago, as Australia moved northward over a mantle hot spot, this now buried, relict landscape contained gold-rich old riverbeds that are not contiguous; the economic mining of these placer deposits in 1859 was thus quite haphazard with most of the alluvial mining of such gold concentrated along the banks of Tooloom Creek and the Clarence River below its junction. The following image shows a down-stream view of a possible gold bearing floodplain on the Clarence River at Paddy's Flat.

The Clarence River at Paddy's Flat in 1988
Source: Garry Gatfield, 2024

Gold can still be panned here today, and the remains of alluvial diggings can be seen in the gullies nearby. This image above is of the Clarence River in partial flood around Christmas 1988, and our camp is located in the middle of the photo. Tooloom Creek joins the Clarence upstream about 2km above this point. Remains of the Brisbane Line 'Tank Trap' can be seen in the form of 30 or more concrete pyramids near the bridge, while a few old graves remain on the river flat near the road amongst the big gum trees.

> *From Upper Tooloom down the river to Lower Tooloom, and even on as far as the junction of the river with the Clarence, prospectors were to be seen, and many of them had obtained substantial evidence of the wisdom of their pursuits. The richest alluvium was supposed to lie on the river, about eight miles downstream from the Rise and Shine claim where Mr. Drysdale had also acquired a lease of 10 acres; this lease basically just comprised a large alluvial flat.*

The Cairn's mining consultant who described the poorly exploited gold from Joe's Gully was writing as an experienced mining engineer and prospector, who had investigated these areas of Joe's Gully and Lower Tooloom. He also confirmed that the Tooloom goldfield was known in the later part of the 1800s for its nuggety gold and he further estimated that Joe's Gully still held a likely gold reserve of $1. 74 million in c1990.

The geology and mining of Lower Tooloom Creek:

This was an existing alluvial mine that harvested old relict, river-gravel deposits from the Permian-Triassic, basalt-capped, Tooloom hillsides. This is the same area mentioned above as Mr. Drysdales' 10 acre lease from the 1860s. This mine also collected and treated wash from redeposited alluvial gravels in existing gullies. The gold found there lacked fines and had a shotty to small nugget size (up to four ounces). This mine had been operating in the early 1990s for two years when this mining consultant from Cairns had evaluated that its economic value was still around $44.5 million.

There was, however, a problem associated with this story that was not of the making of the Cairns mining consultant. There were quite a few mentions of gold from under the heading 'Tertiary basalt cap at Tooloom', in the book written by Thomson (1976) on the 'Geology of the Drake 1:100000 Sheet'. The following passage is a case example:

> *Cappings of Tertiary basalts cover about 80 km^2 in the northwestern part of the Drake Sheet. They unconformably overlie the Mesozoic sediments of the Clarence Moreton Basin (Thomson et al., 1976 p. 105).'*

Jane - my contributing editor had been concerned that she could not conclusively identify basalt outcrops in the field and had begun consulting other sources re their actual existence. The designated sediments certainly were volcanic in nature but these so-called Tertiary volcanics appeared to be more deeply weathered than was likely for Tertiary-aged igneous sediments. Jane suspected a Late Permian and/or Triassic Mesozoic age. This was later confirmed by the work of two separate teams of researchers who were able to utilise the latest Shrimp dating program at the Australian National University in Canberra for two independent papers presented at the NEO Conference in 1999.

Reports on the latter strata that were issued by Thomson (1976). Roberts and Geeve (1999) and Greentree and Flood (1999) were both separately able to confirm that the so-called tertiary deposits on the Emu Creek Block were not different at all to a layer of the same Late Permian and/or Late Triassic sediments that were known to be characteristic of the southern NEO on the Emu Creek Block during the Mesozoic Triassic. The volcanics within the said strata were certainly similar to the Late Palaeozoic and Early Mesozoic but were made up of a mixture of various igneous rocks rather than being just one similar strata and were about 200 Ma older than the tertiary basalts. These were effectively preserving a paleo landscape under the said basalts. It would thus be expected that any gully draining off this area into the Clarence River would erode this old alluvium during heavy runoff conditions today.

The slope down to the creek in Doctor's Gully on the eastern side of Tooloom Creek had no signs of any tertiary lava flows but the alluvial wash was made up of a weathered conglomerate deposit, eroding down the ridge line. Gold can be found in such late Palaeozoic and early Mesozoic deposits of orogen gold as explained further in Chapter 13.

The Tooloom gold rush began to subside after 1862:

The main Tooloom gold rush had effectively run its course by mid-1862 as the view developed amongst the miners that most of the good alluvial gold was then worked out; a steady stream of gold was, however, harvested by a few old timers on the Tooloom field for quite a few years.

Other gold rushes had attracted Tooloom diggers after 1860; these included the rush to Kiandra and the Snowy mountains in early 1860 and the big rush to Gympie in late 1867. The major rush to the Palmer River in North Queensland in 1873 also depleted the miners ranks in Tooloom and from the other Clarence River goldfields.

James Nash mined at Tooloom and McLeod's Creek
Source: State Library Qld. posed in 1890

James Nash of Gympie fame was a digger at Tooloom, he arrived after walking 600 miles from the diggings in central New South Wales. When news of the big rush to Kiandra broke out in early 1860, he along with a number of other Tooloom diggers packed up their tools and swags, caught the steamer from Grafton to Sydney, then walked overland to Kiandra. Upon arrival, he along with numerous other diggers found the rush had been 'overblown' by the newspapers and storekeepers.

Despite this, he spent 5 months at Kiandra before he turned around and walked back to the coast at Merimbula, where he then caught the steamer to Sydney. By 1863 or 64, Nash had moved across the border to the new colony of Queensland, in his quest for gold. History records that he found the fabulous Gympie Goldfield in October 1867; this discovery is credited with saving the young colony of Queensland from bankruptcy.

Many miners had also moved on locally within the Clarence River Catchment to places like Pretty Gully or returned to McLeod's Creek and Timbarra, only to find that the Chinese had bought up all the good claims on both those fields. Small rushes within the Clarence district also occurred at the Bulldog and Ewingar and at Lunatic near Drake.

The NSW Mining Warden Reports in the 1870s recorded a minor revival of interest in gold mining at Tooloom with the application of some mechanised mining on this field. Two large races had been built to overcome the seasonal water shortage problem and some small companies had begun crushing quartz from reefs in the area; most activities were, however, still being restricted by the chronic water shortage on this goldfield. In 1879, the Pioneer Mine was operating a water-wheel and a 5 head stamper at Tooloom and was still employing fifteen miners in 1879.

Few prospectors remained at Tooloom by the 1890s but then there was at least one last hurrah with a rich and unexpected gold find in 1891. This was the remarkable case of John Payne's 'Rise & Shine Gold Mine' that was located adjacent to Joe's Gully.

John Payne's discovery of the 'Rise & Shine Mine' at Tooloom in 1891:

In 1891, John Payne and his son Jack had been prospecting for gold in the gullies and creeks around Drake but, by Christmas of that year, Payne and his son had moved on to the abandoned gullies of Tooloom. They decided to prospect a shaft that Kenny Mclean had abandoned above Joe's Gully and, after clearing out the rubbish in the bottom of the shaft, Jack found rich, gold-reef specimens. Employing only a primitive pestle and mortar dolly, they produced 130ozs of gold from the reef face, and more, after following the reef for a further 130 ft. John Payne then established a new claim on this old shaft area and floated a new mining venture in Brisbane, which he called the 'Rise & Shine Gold Mining Company' at Tooloom. This initally proved to be a very rich find and, within six weeks, they had produced a staggering 600 ounces of gold from their new claim.

It has, however, since been said by Wilkinson (1980: p. 119) that after all the money that was spent on new machinery for the Rise & Shine Mine, insufficient gold was found to pay for it!

These following excerpts from a newspaper clipping in September 1891 also threw further light on Mr. John Payne's gold discovery and the following interview between John Payne and the reporter painted a truly dazzling picture of it.

Prospectus.

For Public Information Only.

PROSPECTUS AND REPORT OF

THE RISE & SHINE GOLD MINING CO.

(NO LIABILITY.)

TOOLOOM, N.S.W.

DIRECTORS :—

HON. B. B. MORETON, Brisbane.
J. H. DAVIDSON, Esq. (Grazier) Brisbane.
E. B. BAKER, Esq. (Grazier) Brisbane.
JAMES GULLAND, Esq. (Gentleman) Brisbane.
W. L. STEVENSON, Esq. (Grazier) Brisbane.

The Shares in the above Company having been applied for, the following Prospectus and Report is published for private information only.

The Capital of the Company is £30,000 divided into 60,000 Shares of 10s. each—17,500 of the said Shares are fully paid up to 10s. each. 35,000 of the said Shares paid up to 9s. each, and contributing to the extent of 10s. per Share, balance 1s. per Share, payable at calls not exceeding 3d. per Share per month, and 7500 contributing Shares to be held in reserve.

The objects for which the Company is established are as follows :—

To purchase, acquire and work certain leasehold lands comprised and held under mineral leases 25, 44, 45, making a total area of 16 acres, situated in the country of Buller, Parish of Clarence, in the colony of New South Wales.

Together with such other deeds and stipulations as are contained in the articles of association of the said Company registered in the office of the Supreme Court of Queensland as a "No Liability Company," under the Company's Act, 1863, the 16th day of May, 1891. Registered Office of the Company, New Zealand Chambers, Brisbane. R. Falkiner, Legal Manager.

The Prospectus for the float of the 'Rise and Shine Gold Mining Co.'
Source: via Trove, 2024

The Warwick Examiner and Times (1867-1919)

The Tooloom Goldfields. Wed. Sept 9, 1891

This is a story of rich reefs on an alluvial goldfield as told by Mr John Payne on his recent trip to Brisbane.

Mr. John Payne was the original proprietor of the 'Rise and Shine' gold-mining claim at Tooloom; he was an old digger of 20 years' experience in all parts of Australia and, in the course of an interview with a representative of this journal, the conversation speedily turned to Tooloom - a new goldfield near the southern border of Queensland in which so much Brisbane money had already been invested. A good deal of information was elicited from Mr. Payne concerning the claims upon, not this new, but rather, revived goldfield.

Tooloom was an old gold field, when some of the richest claims in New South Wales and Queensland sprang into existence and, at one time, it was said that as many as 18,000 (unlikely) men were to be found in the district. This country was regarded as payable gold-bearing country for about 270 square miles. In every gully and every waterhole, gold was to be found and, with systematic working, there was no doubt that the alluvial diggings of Tooloom must and would have, promised a big and profitable future for them. These diggings were regarded at one time as being quite one of the richest in New South Wales and, as a proof that it was not a mere fossicking ground for wanderers, it may be stated that, some years ago and just about a quarter of a mile below the 'Rise and Shine' claim, the famous Lady Bowen nugget, which had weighed just over 140 ounces, had been taken out.

Writing in '*The Forgotten Country*', Wilkinson (1980: p. 119) also recorded that after John Payne had made his money on gold and on the sale of shares in the 'Rise & Shine' Mine, he became very intent on re-establishing the old Tooloom goldfields; this first entailed building a great new house of 14 rooms. This building was constructed with fine red cedar planks that were sourced and milled locally and, after its completion in 1895, it was granted a hotel license and became the Tooloom Hotel. This can still be seen in Tooloom today as a B&B.

John Payne ran a 5-head, stamper mill at Tooloom in 1899 and was also the owner of additional mining claims at Tooloom, registered in 1898, 1899 and in 1904.

Tooloom after 1900:

World Wars I and II saw a marked decline in mining at Tooloom as many of the diggers left the area to enlist in the war effort but the years of the Great Depression, which had commenced in 1929, had quite the opposite effect on the numbers of miners at Tooloom.

Both Australia and New Zealand had been hit very hard by this major economic downturn and many unemployed diggers then returned to the life that they knew best in order to survive and to support their families. Ion Idriess wrote his classic book – *'Prospecting for Gold'*, in 1931 and his first print run was sold out in hours as men took up their picks, their gold pans, and their swags and then headed off for the nearest goldfield that they could find.

This could not, however, happen today as most states have now abolished their Miner's Right; and official gold and mineral fields have now been de-gazetted and available crown land that traditionally allowed small-scale prospecting is now usually off-limits.

Rare wire gold from the Clarence River
Source: Garry Gatfield, 2024

12

A brief geological history of the southern New England Orogen

Readers should consult the *Geological terminology* list in the appendices at the back of this book for assistance with complex geological definitions. Unfortunately, there is no easy way to write the history of gold at Tooloom without using scientific and geological definitions. I have endeavoured to keep my explanations of these terms simple.

Introduction:

An orogen is a geological term for a mountain-building zone and, from at least the Silurian-Devonian in the Middle Palaeozoic to the end of the Mesozoic Triassic, the southern New England Orogen (or southern NEO) was a tectonically-active part of the north-eastern, coastal zone of ancient Gondwanaland. This NEO stretched nearly 1600 kms from Bowen in North Queensland to Newcastle in the Hunter Valley of New South Wales. The NEO has been arbitrarily divided into northern and southern sections at the Queensland-New South Wales border (Hoy et al., 2014). It is planned to confine the present analysis of the east coast New England Orogen to just the southern section, which includes the New England Fold Belt in the present-day area of north-eastern New South Wales.

The western margin of the New England Fold Belt is defined by the Sydney-Gunnedah-Bowen Basin with the north-south Peel-Manning Fault System and the accretionary Tablelands Complex lying to the east of the latter. The Peel Manning Fault System is a tectonic divisor that separates the Tamworth Belt in the west from the accretionary Tablelands Complex to the east (Rosenbaum, 2012, Hoy et al., 2014 and Jessop et al., 2018). See the following Figure 4. for the major structural units (or tectonic sub-divisions) of this north-eastern New England Fold Belt during the southern NEO.

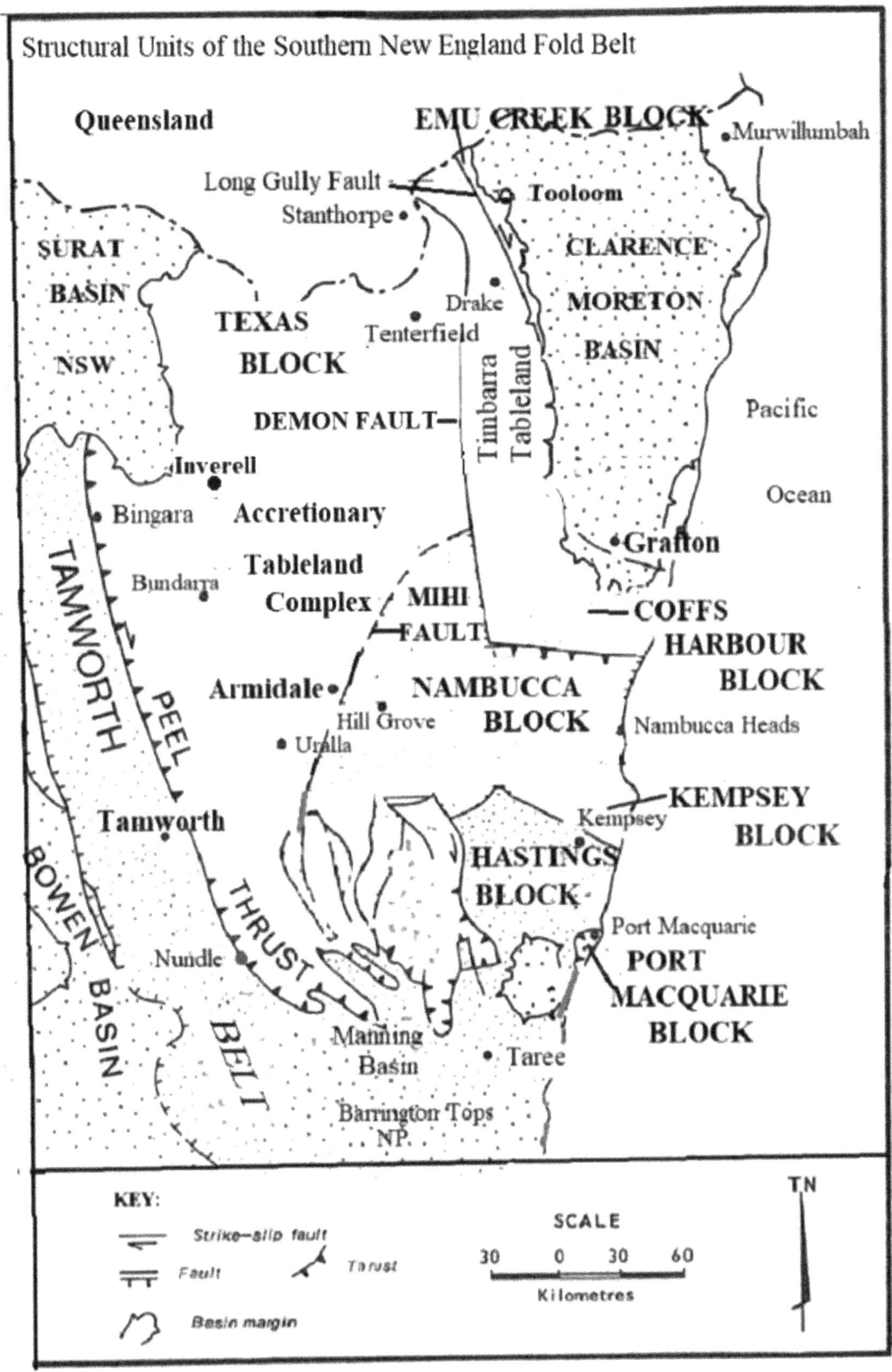

Figure 4. A tectonic subdivision of the Tooloom area in the southern NEO
Source: Adapted from Scheibner, 1974. J.Eberhardt 2024

From at least the end of the Palaeozoic Silurian at approximately 420 million years ago (or at ~420 Ma), the north-eastern margin of Gondwanaland was believed to have become an accretional (but not collisional) shoreline after the pre-Palaeozoic breakup of an earlier continent - Rodinia, in the pre-Pacific, Iapetus Ocean to the east (Meert and Torsvik, 2003 and Rosenbaum, 2018).

Readers might now be asking where the plate tectonics-associated fold mountains are today or were in this region? These did not exist for it is now believed that, although the subduction processes in these accretional subduction zones might not have the plate collisions that produced mountains elsewhere, subduction can still involve tectonic forces such as deformation, compression, oroclinal bending, metamorphism and magmatism (Li et al., 2014). This subduction zone in north-eastern New South Wales is now seen to have been a part of a recycling process of the Gondwanan crustal margin from the Palaeozoic Silurian to the end of the Mesozoic Triassic (Rosenbaum, 2018).

Terrane accretion for the southern NEO:

A 'terrane' is an interesting structural feature of the very complex geology of this north-eastern New England Fold Belt. This term 'terrane' generally refers to an accreted block from elsewhere and describes a discrete, fault-bounded block that differs from its neighbours in terms of its geology, in its geochronology and in its mineral potential. These terranes cannot be assumed to have shared a common geological history with their neighbours (Flood and Aitcheson, 1993). Such terranes are believed to have accumulated in the southern NEO area after the earlier pre-Palaeozoic break-up of Rodinia when pieces of this earlier continent were then subsequently rafted inshore onto the Gondwanan coastal margin and, from there, to be then moved along strike-slip fault lines in this area before accumulating against the suture line along the Peel Manning Fault System or in the accretionary Tablelands Complex to the east of the latter (Meert and Torsvik, 2003).

Some terranes may also have been developed locally and were then moved to a new location via rifting and/or by movement along the previously-mentioned strike-slip faults such as the Peel, the Jump-up, the Long Gully, and the Demon Faults in the vicinity of the Tooloom and Timbarra goldfields. Flood and Aitcheson (1998) reported that they had already identified eleven such terranes in the accretionary Tablelands Complex. This terrane accretionary process has also been linked to the onset of oroclinal bending, which has produced folds in map view rather than high fold mountains like India's northern Himalayas (Rosenbaum, 2012 and 2018).

The arrival of these terranes were a further complicating factor in the tectonic development of the southern NEO in the Devonian - Late Carboniferous. Line (2011) has suggested (based on U-Pb zircon dating) that one of the oldest terrane ages in the southern NEO gave a date ~388 ±7 Ma; this came from a zircon sourced from the Tacking Point Gabbro at Port Macquarie and, thus indicated a Silurian age for that terrane.

Cycles of 'compression and extension' in the southern New England Orogen:

The 'terrane analysis' model for explaining the tectonic setting of the southern NEO was found to be inadequate for researchers trying to fully explain the complex tectonic evolution of the southern NEO. Terrane accretion was verified as predicted in the accretionary Tableland Complex in the north-eastern New England Fold Belt but their further tectonic role was uncertain (Rosenbaum, 2018). A new explanatory model was required and the theory of 'Cycles of compression and extension' has since been evolved to provide a more comprehensive explanation of the tectonics of this region (Jessop et al., 2018 and Rosenbaum, 2018).

The tectonic setting of the southern NEO is currently seen to have been controlled by two or three periodic cycles of compression and extension (or relaxation) over a west-dipping subduction zone with the subsequent migration onshore and offshore of the position of the subduction trench (Jessop et al., 2018 and Rosenbaum, 2018); both these research groups have emphasised the importance of these alternating subduction cycles in understanding the tectonic evolution of this Gondwanan north-eastern margin of the southern NEO.

A compression cycle involved thrust tectonics to the west along the subducting plate as the arc advanced under compression towards the continental plate. An extension (or crustal relaxation) cycle was alternatively initiated by the retreat of the arc towards the oceanic plate to the east. This induced a thinning of the crust in the backarc area due to subsidence and stretching, which in turn, promoted basin formation and a rise in heat from the mantle below with the consequent melting of the deeply buried sediments that had been trapped within them. This melting then formed S-Type (or sediment-derived) magmas (Jessop et al., 2018).

Rosenbaum (2018) has argued that there were at least three cycles of compression and extension in this region from the Palaeozoic Silurian to the Mesozoic Triassic, whilst Jessop et al., (2018) have identified just two. These compression cycles are thought by Rosenbaum (2012 and 2018), to have occurred in the Silurian, in the Devonian-Carboniferous and from the Middle Permian to the Triassic at ~160 Ma, when Gondwanaland first began to break up and the southern NEO then terminated (Jessop et al., 2018).West-dipping subduction is believed to have begun in the Silurian in the New England Fold Belt:

The westward-dipping subduction trench is believed to have been obducted (see the geological descriptions in the Appendices for a definition of this term) onto the then convergent but not collisional, north-eastern margin of Gondwanaland during the Late Silurian to Middle Devonian. This west-dipping subduction trench was believed to have been activated at ~420 Ma (Jessop et al., 2018 and Rosenbaum, 2018).

The related Late Silurian to Middle Devonian tectonics is understood to have initially included an Andean-style magmatic island forearc and forearc basin margin. This had, however, become a hot continental arc by the Late Devonian. This then remained active over the north-eastern Gondwanan margin until the end of the Carboniferous and the beginning of the Permian (Rosenbaum, 2012 and Hoy et al., 2014). See the cross-section of this NEO subduction zone in the following Figure 5.

Eventually, the presence of this active, west-dipping subduction-trench in this area imposed '*some style of plate tectonics order*' onto this New England Fold Belt area, whereby this subduction zone, with its volcanic arc and related 'hot' backarc area then had a set location within the north-eastern Fold Belt and also had a persistent west-dipping orientation (Glen and Scheibner, 1993 p.125). These authors also suggested that the development of this active but stable Late Devonian-Carboniferous plate-tectonics style of margin then marked the actual onset of the southern New England Orogen.

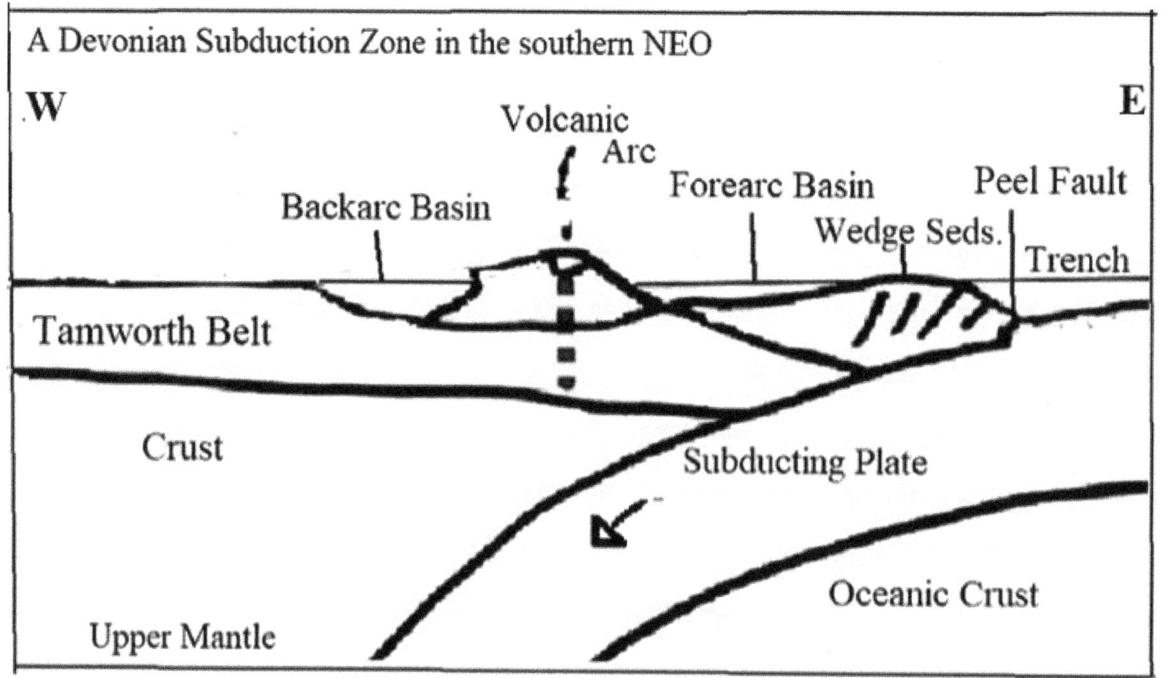

Figure 5. An cross-section of the Devonian subduction zone from Bingara in the West to the Pacific Ocean in the East
Source: J. Eberhardt, 2024

The Emu Creek Block (or terrane) in the Late-Devonian-Carboniferous:

Terranes from the eastern ocean had intruded the accretionary Tablelands Complex of Gondwanaland from the Late Silurian to the end of the Devonian-Carboniferous. The Emu Creek Block has been partially exposed by erosion from under a covering of weathered basalts and now outcrops at the old Tooloom goldfield. This small exposure (of just 45 kms long by 20 kms wide) is a block with a likely Carboniferous depositional age (Hoy et al., 2014) that outcrops on the western edge of the Clarence-Moreton Basin just to the south of the Queensland border.

Terrane accretion to the west and south of Tooloom has been associated with many of the important tectonic processes that have determined this region's great geological complexity. The arrival of terranes in this area inevitably caused some uplift. There was then a consequence increase in the rate of erosion and burial during the Late Carboniferous and much of this increased 'immature' sedimentation accumulated in new sedimentary basins in the Texas Beds area and in the Surat and Clarence-Moreton Basins (Hoy, 2014 p.12).

The sediments of the Emu Creek Block in the Carboniferous:

The volcanic arc was found further to the west in this Late Devonian-Carboniferous period but was well-represented by extrusive andesites and dacites in the sediments of this north-eastern New England Fold Belt. Most Devonian-Carboniferous tectonic units of this time, like the western Tamworth Belt and the accretionary Tablelands Complex, contained extensive forearc basin rocks and volcanoclastic (or pyroclastic) sediments (Hoy et al., 2014).

Buckman et al., (2010 p.87) have described an example of immature volcanic sediments from the Nundle area on the southern section of the Tamworth Belt, which were made up of uncemented and unlayered volcanic breccias and conglomerates. Hoy et al., (2014) have also described the sediments from the Paddy's Flat Formation at Tooloom as *being typically immature with weathered feldspars and volcanoclastic conglomerates* that included andesites and dacites. These are up to 12 metres thick at the top of the succession (Buckman et al., 2010 and Hoy et al., 2014 p.1115). The Emu Creek Block has large areas of immature sediments and extensive layers of cobbled conglomerates in conjunction with thickly-bedded layers of volcanoclastic materials. The previous authors have thus suggested that *the Emu Creek Block was once part of the Carboniferous forearc basin of the southern NEO (Hoy et al., 2014 p.1129).*

The Paddy's Flat formation was younger than, and was overlayed by, the Emu Creek Formation at Tooloom. Hoy et al., (2014, p.1114) has calculated the Emu Creek Block's depositional age as 305.5±1.4 Ma. This places the depositional age of the Paddy's Flat formation at Tooloom at the end of the Late Carboniferous (Encyc. Britannica gives 298.9 Ma as the end of the Carboniferous and the beginning of the Early Permian).

McKay and Wake (2015) have reported a similar occurrence of such conglomerates and breccias on the Emu Creek Block at Tooloom and this can also be observed in a South Tooloom road-cutting on the interfluve between Pretty Gully and Doctor's Gully close to Lanakai. Such immature sediments permitted the easy infiltration of hydrothermal, gold-containing fluids during times of compression and uplift in the Devonian-Carboniferous. The 'golden gullies' of Tooloom and of the Phoenix area further to its north, appear have been affected by eruptions of basalts, andesites, dacites and rhyolites and by the infiltration of the previously-mentioned gold-carrying, hydrothermal fluids from their coarser-grained deep-seated, intrusive equivalents such as gabbro, diorite, granodiorite and granite in this area in the Devonian-Carboniferous. This was most likely to have been the source of the gold at places like Joe's Gully at Tooloom (McKay and Wake, 2015).

There is also strong evidence from this small exposure of the Emu Creek Block at the Tooloom goldfield that this area had been affected by at least two events of regional compression and folding during the Devonian-Late Carboniferous (Hoy et al., 2014 and Rosenbaum, 2012). At Paddy's flat near Tooloom, folds that were produced by the compressional forces of the Late Carboniferous are open and steeply inclined; the associated Emu Creek Block folds at Tooloom are also steeply inclined but are asymmetrical (Hoy et al., 2014).

The rocks of the accretionary Tablelands Complex in the Late Carboniferous have also provided further evidence that this was still a time of compression. These rocks are typically deep-marine, volcaniclastic turbidites with mafic, volcanic rocks, mudflow deposits, and even some limestone (Hoy et al., 2014). These Carboniferous rocks also show signs of mild metamorphic conditions including prehnite-pumpellyite/lower greenschist to amphibolite-facies in addition to an exposure of serpentinites, blue schists and eclogites (Rosenbaum, 2012 and Buckman et al., 2010).

The geochronology of the sediments of the Emu Creek Block on the eastern side of the Peel Manning Fault System similarly show a strong resemblance to the Carboniferous sediments of the western Tamworth Belt at this time. These resemble the detritus of a forearc basin such as was found in the latter (Hoy et al, 2014 p.1120).

Diorite and granodiorite clasts from the southern NEO, which contain xenoliths of basalts, further indicate that the on-going magmatism of the Late Carboniferous and Early Permian was bimodal. This author (Garry) has previously shown me a large clast of diorite that contained a large black xenolith of basalt, which came from the stream bed of the Timbarra River. Garry assures me that such specimens are quite common there and in the creeks in that area. Buckman et al., have determined from these that rifting was likely to have been occurring in that same Late Carboniferous period (Buckman et al., 2010). Such clasts with basalt-xenoliths are thus indicative of rifting-induced bimodal magmatism (Shaanan et al., 2015).

Such magmatism is said to have occurred when it was produced by the eruption of both felsic and mafic magmas from a single volcanic source without the production of an intermediate magma. This type of magmatism was usually associated with backarc extension conditions and this was known to be characterised by the development of rift basins (Rosenbaum et al., 2012 p.3 and Jessop et al., 2018 p.4). The emplacement of these S-type granitoids (from melted sediments) was believed to have occurred simultaneously with the advent of rifting in the southern NEO (Shaanan et al., 2015. p.7).

Shallow, felsic, intrusive rocks had formed a basement to the sediments of the Emu Creek Block and the Tamworth Belt by the beginning of the Carboniferous. These rocks were then overlain by a variety of volcanoclastic (or pyroclastic) flow sediments (Hoy et al., 2014).

Zircon U_Pb dating and a similarity of common ice-age type fossils (*from the Levipustula Levis faunal assemblage*) has also since linked the Emu Creek Block to an origin in the Tamworth Belt (Hoy et al., 2014). This area of Gondwanaland was believed to have been located at or near the South Pole at this time.

The Permian cycle of extension at ~300 Ma:

The mild compression of the Late Carboniferous had ceased by the beginning of the Permian and a new phase of back-arc extension began at ~300-285 Ma. This was likely again linked to the retreat of the subduction zone towards the oceanic plate to the east (Rosenbaum, 2018).

The Devonian-Carboniferous volcanic arc, its forearc basin and its later 'hot' continental, backarc basin and along with the associated accretionary complexes to its east had already provided the major tectonic foundations for the southern New England Orogen by the beginning of the Early Permian (Jessop et al., 2018).

The crustal stretching and consequent thinning that accompanied this new phase of backarc extension allowed these sediments in the new sedimentary basins to sink and melt; both S-Type (dominant) and I-Type (minor) granitoids were then emplaced at ~298 to 288 Ma (Rosenbaum, 2018). This author has also noted that this was a time when both backarc extension and oroclinal bending had already begun.

Both these types of granitoids were emplaced at the same time in a curved belt that followed the later outline of the Texas and Manning oroclines (Rosenbaum et al., 2012, 2018 and Li et al., 2014). The Early Permian granitoids (mainly S-Type) were generally unfractionated and reduced. There was some tin and wolfram mineralisation associated with the S-Type granites but these were not as important as were the later emplacements of the metal-rich I-Type and leucogranites in the Middle-Late Permian and in the Mesozoic-Triassic (Ford et al., 2019).

The dominant S-Type granitoids of the Early Permian at ~298-288 Ma came from the Bundarra Granite Super Suite (Rosenbaum et al., 2012). These S-Type granites were not rich in metals like the I-Type granites but some of these are now known to have hosted some tin and Molybdenum mineral systems and some gold with or without stibnite (Ford et al., 2019). This claim of tin from S-Type granites has been quite difficult to verify in the literature.

The I-Type granitoids came, however, from mafic, basaltic magmas that were sourced in the upper mantle during rifting (Buckman et al., 2010).

The development of deep sedimentary basins continued throughout the Early Permian, with the emplacement of the granitoids and the formation of the Texas and Coffs Harbour oroclines in the period 300-260 Ma. These, with the continuation of bimodal magmatism, the associated rifting and the developing oroclines became important tectonic characteristics of the southern NEO in the Early Permian (Rosenbaum et al., 2012 and 2018).

The 'Quiet time' at the end of the Early Permian when magmatism ceased:

The bimodal magmatism of the Early Permian ceased at ~280 Ma for a period of 20 to 25million years with the onset of a quiet period (Rosenbaum, 2020) before magmatism resumed again at ~265 Ma with compression and deformation in the Middle Permian:

The Hunter Bowen Orogeny and the intrusion of the metalliferous I-Type granitoids:

Mild compression resumed again in the Middle Permian until the onset of a broader period of strong compression. This was known as the Hunter Bowen Orogeny, which affected both the northern and southern NEO and which augmented the local and milder compressional effects already in place. The Hunter Bowen Orogeny affected the whole New England Orogen in the period ~265 to 230 Ma and in the Late Permian to the Early to Middle Triassic (Rosenbaum, 2018). From the Middle to the Late Permian at ~265 Ma) and then to the Upper Triassic at ~235 Ma, the New England Orogen was thus again subjected to pronounced east-west contractional deformation (Rosenbaum (2018) and to widespread I-type calc-alkaline and felsic to intermediate intrusions (McKay and Wake, 2015).

This time, the granitoids being emplaced during this period of crustal shortening after ~265 Ma were more likely to be the metal-bearing I-Type magmas from the Clarence River Supersuite as in the Jenny Lind granite at Tooloom or the K-rich leucogranites of the Moombi Suite as at Timbarra, where gold was disseminated in the roof -zone of the intrusion (McKay and Wake, 2015 and Mustard et al., 2001).

The prevailing magmatism was again bimodal and this resulted in intrusion-related I-type mineral systems based on tin, wolfram, gold and molybdenum during the late Permian (at 259–251 Ma) in the Early to Middle Triassic (250 to ~230 Ma) and in the Late Triassic ~230 Ma. These I-Type magmas were particularly significant for the origin of the gold at Tooloom and at associated goldfields of this north-eastern fold belt region.

The S-Type granites usually produced granodiorites and tonalites but these were not known for their great fertility in the southern NEO area (Chappell et al. 2012). Magmatism in the southern NEO at this time meant that detritus from this magmatism was deposited into the new rift-related sedimentary basins (Rosenbaum, 2012).

While some modest mineralisation (of molybdenum, copper, wolfram, bismuth and gold) was associated with the Permian Moonbi Supersuite, significant granite-related mineralisation has been more or less deemed to be only associated with the Triassic leucogranites. These leucogranites comprised the most important group of mineralised granites in the southern NEO and have produced tin, wolfram, molybdenum, silver, arsenic, bismuth, copper, lead, gold, fluorite, beryl and topaz (Blevin, 2010).

This late Permian-Triassic magmatism, which continued until ~230 Ma, was again related to continental arc magmatism with the re-establishment of a west-dipping subduction zone and the new sedimentary rift basins in this area. Slab break-off and subsequent rollback may also have been operating at this time with a retreat of the subduction zone to the east again (Jessop et al., 2018 and Rosenbaum et al., 2018). This bimodal volcanic activity reached a peak in the period 265-250 Ma; the intrusion of granitoids then likely ceased soon after ~250 Ma with the subduction zone thought to have again retreated offshore to the east, thus bringing the Hunter-Bowen compressional cycle to an end in the southern NEO.

The Triassic Late Extension cycle and the end of the southern NEO:

Following a return to an extension cycle in the Late Triassic after the Hunter Bowen compressional cycle finished around 210 Ma, Gondwanaland began to break apart; Australia and New Zealand started to split from Antarctica due to rifting by -160 Ma (Jessop et al., 2018) and Australia from New Zealand by ~125 Ma; the Tasman Sea also began to open by ~80 Ma (Jessop et al., 2018).

Conclusion:

In the words of some of the our previous authors, the southern NEO has thus been identified as a Devonian-Carboniferous:

> *Convergent margin complex comprising forearc basin rocks of the Tamworth Belt, with correlative terranes and accretionary meta-sedimentary rocks of the Tablelands Complex, which are separated from each other by a tectonic contact in the Peel Manning Fault System (Rosenbaum, 2012 p.187) .*

Another way of thinking about the tectonic processes going on at this same time in the southern NEO from the Late Devonian to the end of the Triassic was also provided by Li et al., *(2014) as:*

> *'The NEO was a subduction-related orogen that developed in the Late Devonian-Carboniferous and was modified in the Permian by deformation, by magmatism and by oroclinal bending (Li et al., 2014 p.20).*

Figure 6. The New England Fold Belt in the NEO
Source: Adapted from Mackay and Wake, 2015. Garry Gatfield, 2024

13

Sources of gold in the southern New England Orogen

In his 1931 book - *Prospecting for Gold,* well-known author and prospector - Ion Idriess, recommended that Australians should seek gold in 'Serpentine country'. He was not wrong! Gold is hosted by the Great Serpentinite Belt that outcrops along the edge of the Tamworth Belt at Bingara. Additional areas of weathered Permian and Early Triassic basalts with evidence of cobbles and conglomerates are also likely to be a good locality for gold fossicking, if you can get permission! (This is based on this editor's own humble opinion after having researched this above section).

Orogenic gold in the southern NEO:

Groves et al., (1998) have argued that the so-called mesothermal gold deposits of places like the southern New England Orogen were a 'special case' that should instead be called 'orogenic gold'. These authors considered that these 'special gold deposits' were formed in compression cycles during the deformational processes. These were associated with the accretionary plate margins of orogens such as the southern NEO during the Palaeozoic. Special conditions were initially attached by Groves et al., to such orogenic gold deposits; these were to be major vein systems that were associated with regionally metamorphosed terranes or with low sulphide, subduction-related thermal events that would raise the geothermal gradient of the gold deposit episodically to drive

long-distance hydrothermal and (gold-carrying) fluid migration (Groves et al., 1998).

These same authors also expected that the depths of gold deposition for these ore bodies would be quite variable and have suggested that such deposition could vary from a near surface gold deposit to a depth of up to 20 kms and, further, that most of these gold deposits might even be post-orogenic at the time of their emplacement.

A number of other authors have also subscribed to this concept of orogenic gold. These authors have included Goldfarb, 2001: Lewis and Downes, 2008: Wyman et al., 2016 and Groves, 2019. There are, however, still some ongoing issues in the recognition of such systems in relation to the likely sources of the gold-bearing fluids for such gold deposits. Groves et al., (2019) have now answered this problem:

> *All hydrothermal gold deposits are shown to be related in that they formed progressively during the evolution of subduction-related processes along convergent margins. Porphyry-related systems that are formed initially from magmatic hydrothermal fluids are related to the melting of fertile mantle to initiate calc alkaline to high K felsic magmatism in volcanic arcs directly related to subduction.'* (Source: Groves et al., 2019 p.2).

Groves (2019) has since dropped his initial requirement that orogenic gold needs to be associated with gold in metamorphosed terranes. Of particular interest at Tooloom are the possible Intrusion-Related-Gold-Deposits (IRGDs) of the Emu Creek Block in and around the Tooloom Goldfield, the Timbarra Tableland and around other goldfields to the south of Tooloom.

There are possible orogenic gold deposits at Tooloom:

Orogenic intrusions form during or after an orogeny and, via their associated hydrothermal fluids, produce predictable zonation patterns of minerals (including gold plus or minus stibnite) around the intrusions; these are to be found on the inboard side of a convergent shoreline as happened in the southern New England Orogen from the Palaeozoic Middle Devonian to the end of the Mesozoic Triassic (Groves et al., 1998). These orogenic intrusions are low in sulphides, which distinguishes them from other copper and gold-related mineral systems. Major faults and even smaller shear zones not only allow the circulation of hydrothermal fluids that carry the gold but they also control the emplacement of these orogenic structures. Gold-enriched fluid movement around a granitoid or an IRGD intrusion can be laterally extensive if the area of emplacement has many small faults as in the Carboniferous period at and near Tooloom on the Emu Creek Block (Geoscience Australia. Sect. 2, 2023).

The I-Type granites that intruded the accretionary Tablelands Complex in the Permian in the southern NEO included much hydrothermal gold plus or minus stibnite (or antimony) deposits (Stroud, 1999).

Australian orogenic granites are usually polymetallic and have a predictable pattern of zoned minerals around them with elevated levels of gold, silver, molybdenum, bismuth, arsenic, pyrites, and antimony (or stibnite) as at Tooloom and at Timbarra (Mustard, 2001 and McKay, 2015). Australian IRGD deposits usually produce only low grades of gold although there has been one notable exception to this generalisation - the now-closed Kidson gold mine in Queensland.

Another IRGD - Gold in the roof zone of a granitoid on Timbarra Tableland:

The Timbarra goldfield is found on Timbarra Tableland in the headwaters of the Clarence River at a distance of 15 kms to the southeast of Tenterfield and 25 kms to the southwest of Drake. It also lies to the south of our fossicking interest area at Tooloom.

Collectively, the I-type leucogranites of Timbarra, Stanthorpe and Ruby Greek all belong to the most economically significant granite group in the southern New England Orogen-the Moombi Super Group, and these granites are highly fractionated and are heavily mineralised (Stroud, et al., 1999).

The Timbarra Tableland is located within a Palaeozoic s ubduction-related accretionary complex of oceanic crustal terranes (Cohen and Dunlop, 2004).

Alluvial and colluvial gold was first discovered at Timbarra around 1857 and, by the end of that year, rich alluvial deposits were being mined along McLeod's Creek on the northern side of the Timbarra Tableland. Water for sluicing was always scarce on this goldfield and the use of the sluicing method to wash the gold meant that this activity had to be done in the only three months of the year when rainfall was expected to be sufficient for this endeavour. Gold mining became significant in this area after 1857, when good gold was found at Poverty Point high on a spur on the western side of the Timbarra River and on the southern side of McLeod's Creek (Cohen and Dunlop, 2004).

The gold in this area occurs as small, coarse-grained colluvium in the shallow, surface soil and in the weathered granitic layers in the roof-zone of the intrusive pluton. Many miners were successful and this area of Timbarra was proclaimed a goldfield in May 1859. McQueen (2018) and Mustard et al., (2001) have described how there were five main deposits of gold at Timbarra, which were disseminated in the roof zone of a highly fractionated and low-magnetic leucogranite that had cored the barren, monzogranite host (Mustard 2001).

The goldfields at Timbarra, as at Tooloom in 1859, were essentially alluvial in nature. This pluton has been eroded to produce alluvial gold and this gold is also found in the granitic detritus or colluvium on the steeper slopes and as alluvium in the creeks that flowed off the Tableland. These streams trended mainly to the north-east due to faulting in the granitic pluton, before flowing back into Timbarra Creek, which was also called the Rocky River. This pattern of localised gold mineralisation from just beneath the cap of this pluton was also determined by the multitude of faults, joints and cooling fractures in the roof zone itself (Mustard, 2001). The largest pieces of disseminated gold at Timbarra were about the size of a small fingernail (Garry Gatfield, Pers. Comm. 22nd Sept. 2023). There were few nuggets found on this gold field. These coarse granites accounted for the bulk of the gold that was produced from the Timbarra Tableland and the rest came from gold-bearing dykes or veins in this same area (Mustard, 2001 and Stroud et al, 1999).

Mustard described the gold-bearing granitic intrusion at Timbarra as a:

Texturally complex, zoned pluton (Mustard, 2001).

The Timbarra gold deposits have now been classed as a meta-hydrothermal type of the newly recognised Intrusion-Related-Gold-Deposit or IRGD. Stroud et al., (1999) have described how such disseminated gold deposits plus or minus stibnite in the upper 240 m of the Timbarra pluton were quite common in the southern New England Fold Belt.

A leucogranite core, which has intruded the monzogranite at Timbarra, is an I-type felsic granite that has been highly fractionated and has been disseminated by muscovite-chlorite-carbonate alteration (Mustard, 2001). It has a very low sulphide concentration of <1% (Porter Geo

Consultancy, 2001), plus a mineralisation pattern that began with quartz and K-feldspar and has finished with arsenopyrite, pyrite, fluorite and molybdenite, and also producing a final assemblage of muscovite, chlorite, gold, calcite, silver-bismuth, telluride, lead-bismuth and, sometimes, galena and chalcopyrite (Porter Geo Consultancy, 2001 and Mustard, 2001).

This pattern of disseminated gold, which is found here at Timbarra, is unusual by comparison to other known intrusion-related gold systems but this area has already been so recognised as an IRGD and this zonation pattern of other base minerals with the gold and the very low level of sulphur in the deposit is very characteristic for the descriptions of the newly recognised 'intrusion-related and orogenic gold deposit systems'.

The influence of faulting on orogenic gold deposits in the southern NEO:

Much of the known gold and stibnite deposits in the southern NEO are now recognised as being structurally controlled by the many major and smaller faults on the Emu Creek Block. These include the Peel Manning Fault System with the parallel Demon and Jump-up faults to the west of Tooloom and by the Long Gully fault in close proximity to it but lying to the east of the Tooloom area. There is also the intrusion-related gold system that is now identified at Timbarra and, possibly now, also at Tooloom and Phoenix; these latter are gold deposits that were shed from felsic Devonian - Late Carboniferous and Permian dykes.

Terranes such as the Emu Creek block (now renamed the 'Gamilaroi terrane' for its origin in the Tamworth Belt) in this area close to or at Tooloom have generally been described as fault-bounded blocks. Their arrival in this area of the southern New England Fold Belt during the Devonian-Carboniferous has had significant consequences for our discovery of gold here. Terrane boundaries and gold discoveries have been shown to coincide with most of the major fault lines in this north-eastern corner of New South Wales (Flood and Aitcheson, 1993). The associated tectonic processes of faulting, folding, and the accretion of terranes has assisted in the emplacement of rich gold resources in this region (Geoscience Aust. Sect.2, 2023). There are many such small un-mapped faults in the Tooloom area that still remain covered today by sedimentation from the Clarence Moreton Basin.

In the southern NEO, the occurrence of the previously-mentioned oroclinal bending and compression has undoubtedly also helped to produce a favourable environment for allowing the intrusion of mantle materials that can also contain gold-bearing fluids in addition to the serpentinites. The Ion Idress advice thus may be correct in such a case. The Great Serpentinite Belt is certainly renown for positive gold mineralisation along the eastern edge of the Tamworth Belt and in the Coffs Harbour orocline on the eastern side of this block in the southern NEO.

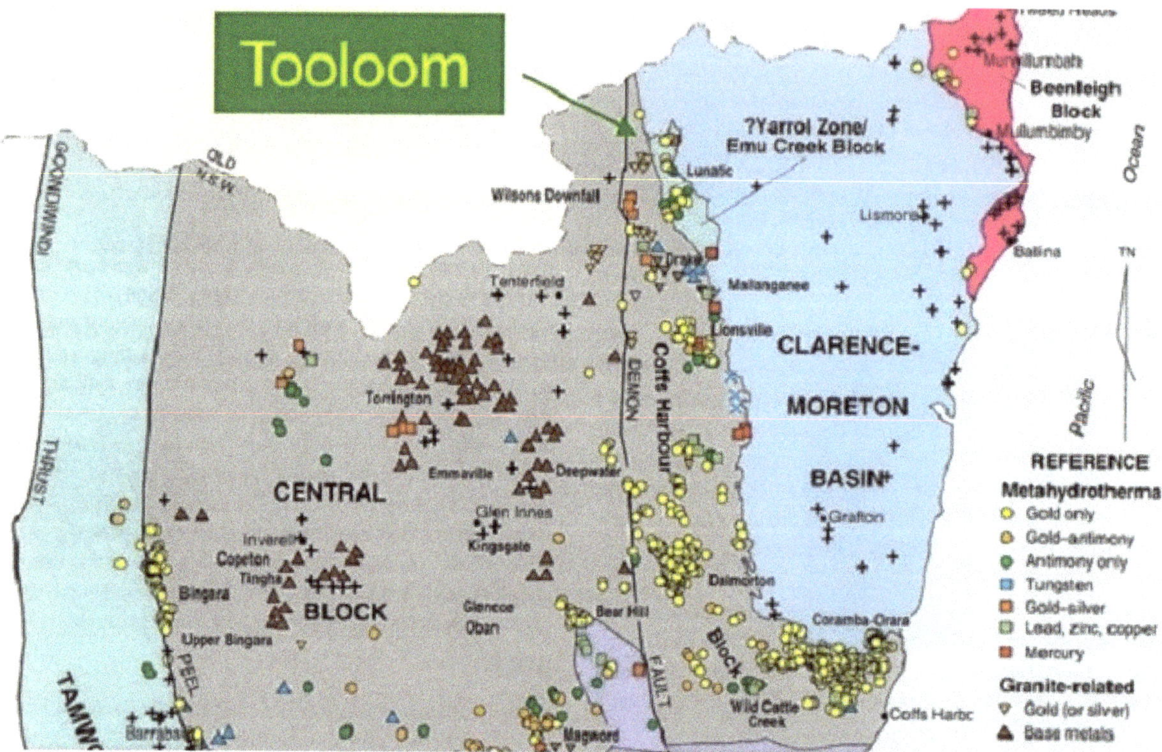

Figure 7. Faulting constrains gold deposits from Tooloom to Coffs Harbour
Source: Adapted from Samso, 2024

A pattern of gold mineralisation between the Demon and Long Gully Faults at Timbarra:

Garry Gatfield – the author of this book, drew this editor's attention to a very interesting pattern in the previous Figure 7. The gold mineralisation, as denoted by the small yellow circles, mainly occur between two major fault lines with fewer known gold deposits to the west of the Demon Fault or to the east of the Long Gully fault until you reach the Peel Manning Fault System much further to the west. The density of previous gold finds and of old, small, mining townships is also highest between these fault lines where they wrap around the southern end of the Coffs Harbour block. These faults follow the approximate line of bending of the Coffs Harbour Orocline and delineate an extension of the Great Serpentinite Belt in this area.

Letter to this Editor,
11th September, 2023

One of the most interesting and important features of the gold deposits of the Clarence River Catchment is the way that they basically lie in a north/south alignment and are bordered on the west by the Demon Fault and on the east by the Long Gully Fault Line.

This north/south alignment commences just over the Queensland Border at a small auriferous outcrop about 10km north of Tooloom and stretches in a direct, southerly line to around Dalmorton, which is situated inland on the old Road from Grafton to Glen Innes.

Commencing at the northern extremity, we can list the important gold fields thus: Tooloom, Paddy's Flat, Pretty Gully, Lunatic, Drake/Mt Carrington, Long Gully/Lady Jersey, McLeod's Creek, Timbarra River and Tableland, Surface Hill/Poverty Point, Malara Creek, Cangai, and Dalmorton.

There are certainly more known gold deposits to the south of Dalmorton, such as the Sara River (south-east. of Glen Innes), Kentucky, and Hillgrove/Metz (near Armidale), all on the same general alignment, but the two major fault lines are no longer visible so they may simply be covered by later sediments on the Coffs Harbour Block or by sediments of the Clarence-Moreton Basin.

There are many more minor fields and deposits that are not listed above and which are enclosed by these two major and regional fault lines. Of course, some deposits are just outside these boundaries, but that doesn't detract from the fundamental importance of these constraints.

Garry Gatfield

The Phoenix Gold Project at Tooloom may be another Intrusion-Related-Gold-Deposit:

In 1997, a gold exploration company - Malachite Resources NL, began looking for gold in the 'Golden Gullies' of the old Tooloom gold field.

The sedimentary rocks of the Tooloom goldfield consists of mainly, gently-folded conglomerates, sandstones, carbonaceous siltstones and tuffs of the Emu Creek Formation. Alluvial gold was found historically in Joe's Gully, at Fraser's and at Cullens Gully. Gold could also be found in narrow, sheeted, quartz veins and in stockworks within the Emu Creek Formation's sedimentary rocks and in areas adjacent to dolerite dykes and felsic intrusions.

As we have previously noted, large nuggets were found in the 'golden gullies' of Tooloom as McKay and Wake (2015) have reported in connection with their recent discoveries of felsic intrusions in these gullies. These intrusions are believed to be connected by dykes to deeper, underlying plutons of granodiorites and granites (McKay and Wake, 2015).

These rocks are also now thought to have been of Devonian-Carboniferous age. The 'golden gullies' were all heavily worked for alluvial gold during the 1859 to 1862 goldrush. This area had, however, been only minimally worked for hard rock gold by way of digging shafts. There are still a few scattered shafts around Tooloom's hillsides today and these were all mainly dug after 1862 (McKay and Wake, 2015).

Gold mineralisation at Tooloom is clearly associated with these newly discovered major intrusion centres. Each of the three previously mentioned gullies - Joe's, Fraser's and Cullen's, is associated with a number of significant gold occurrences, both within and adjacent to, these intrusion complexes.

More work is needed to definitively link these newly discovered mineral systems at Tooloom to the IRGDs model but the style of the mineralisation and the close proximity of the golden gullies to the newly discovered intrusions suggests the formation of magmatic hydrothermal system(s) that are closely related to these intrusions. The Malachite geologists recognised these as being similar to the rare Intrusion-Related-Gold-Deposits Systems or IRGDs, which had recently been found and described in Alaska's and the Yukon's Tintina goldfield (McKay and Wake, 2015). This type of gold deposit is usually a big system; not many such areas have been recognised around the world so far, but Australia already has at least two. One is located at the Kidston Gold Mine area in Northern Queensland and the second is located to the south of Tooloom at Timbarra.

These possible IRGDs in the Tooloom gullies also appear to be very similar to Groves' descriptions of orogenic gold and we will treat them as such for the purposes of this analysis.

The Phoenix Gold Project was another candidate for an IRGD in the Tooloom area after Malachite Resources discovered Phoenix in 2007 by following up on multiple indications of gold in BLEG (leached stream sediment samples) that had been collected just to the north of Tooloom. These led the company to an outcrop of hydrothermal breccia (the Phoenix Breccia); initial gold values from the breccia were, however, very low at 0.2 - 0.4 g/t Au). Such a factor is likely to have been one of the main reasons why this system had lain undiscovered for so many years after 1859.

The Phoenix breccia lies on the northern side of an annular breccia anomaly with a coincident gold-arsenic-antimony-bismuth-copper soil geochemical anomaly that measures at least 1 km in diameter. A second anomaly also extends down to at least 400 m in depth and is equal to approximately one billion tonnes of gold-mineralised rock. These related quartz-biotite and hornfels clastic sedimentary rocks of the Emu Creek Formation are, however, carrying a very low-grade gold mineralisation of only 0.1-0.5 g/t of Au at Phoenix (McKay and Wake, 2015).

Malachite Resources planned to further investigate another soil anomaly along a fault zone that ran south-west from the annular-shaped breccia but, instead, Malachite abandoned their venture at Phoenix in 2018 after failing to find a development partner. The gold yields at Phoenix may have been too low for risk adverse investors. Another negative factor in this decision may also have been related to a further Malachite report that the system was open to the north-east around the annular breccia pipe, which was believed to have been the central mineralising intrusion. Hydrothermal gold cannot accumulate without an effective trap for the gold system.

Despite the risks, there is a clear association here of gold with bismuth, arsenic and antimony (stibnite) at Phoenix where there is mineralisation throughout the breccia and the presence of stibnite, with grades up to 8.3% Sb over 1 m, thus adding significant extra value for any potential miner.

A newly defined tonalite-granodiorite intrusion, known as the 70K Tonalite, has also been mapped at Phoenix. This intrusive lies directly to the northwest of the Phoenix breccia but the breccia pipe itself is thought to be located within the hornfels aureole of a deeper seated, as yet unrecognised, mineralising intrusion (McKay and Wake, 2015). More information on this new discovery may yet stimulate investment here and, already, its general characteristics do seem to correspond to the new knowledge now known about IRGDs or orogenic gold deposits.

Gold was also found in the volcanics at Drake and at Lunatic to the south of Tooloom:

There were a number of small gold fields towards Drake and Timbarra; Pretty Gully and Lunatic are some examples. One such interesting gold deposit in this Southern New England Fold Belt area includes the low-sulphide, epithermal and orogenic gold-deposit that is hosted within volcanic rocks such as the Mt. Carrington complex at Drake, which is a township located about six miles to the north of the Timbarra Tableland (Beeson and Borten, 2015). The particular gold resource at Mt Carrington is contained within an area of intermediate to felsic volcanic rocks of Late Permian age. These volcanics were further intruded by Late Permian to Early Triassic granitoids and by more basic intrusions. The volcanics, which belong to the Wandsworth Volcanic Group, are believed to have been deposited in a shallow, marine environment. This Drake deposit is nearly 400 metres thick (McQueen, 2018 and Beeson and Borten, 2015).

The Mt Carrington gold deposit occurs within an area of low magnetic response, which other researchers have called the 'Drake quiet zone'. The volcanics rocks here include both andesites and volcanic porphyries and these were later intruded by both andesitic and rhyolitic dykes. The Mt Carrington mineral zone has been extensively altered by 'silica-sericite-pyrite' alteration (Beeson and Borten, 2015). These authors have also noted that previous researchers have identified that Mt Carrington sits in the south-western corner portion of what appears to be a volcanic, cauldron-like feature and this, in turn, is nested within the 'Drake quiet zone'. Faulted structures also occur around its margins (Beeson and Borten, 2015).

Epithermal mineralisation occurs along the whole 40 kms length of the Drake Volcanics but Mt Carrington and Red Rock have the richest deposits of altered mineralisation. This deposit is polymetallic for gold, silver, zinc and even some copper; lead can also be found in association with it. The occurrence of such minerals has been controlled by the distribution of the various types of host rocks. The richest gold area is found in Central Mt Carrington within the intermediate to felsic Drake Volcanics (Beeson and Borten, 2015).

This Drake gold deposit was found by a travelling salesman-Sam Costa, who decided to have a quick fossick in a nearby creek during his lunch break (Wilkinson, 1980).

Sam Costa found nothing in the creek but, while having lunch, his eye kept returning to the big and brooding rocks high on a ridge on the other side of the creek and he thought that it was probably worth it to try his luck at gold panning there after lunch. He later scrambled up the slope and did just that. He was not particularly impressed by the grey basaltic rocks but he retrieved some chips, planning to dolly them later for gold and began packing up. He was of two minds as to whether he would even bother to dolly the rock chips but he eventually did so and was rewarded by the sight of some flecks of bright yellow gold in the pan. Feverishly, he then staked out his claim and rushed off to the resident Gold Commissioner to register it.

When Sam Costa told the Commissioner the location of his claim, the latter was openly incredulous.

> *Here in Fairfield? There's never been gold found here abouts. Out at Lunatic and Timbarra ...... but not here at Fairfield! The Commissioner exclaimed (*Fairfield is now Drake) (Source: Wilkinson, 1980).

The Gold Commissioner was wrong and Sam Costa was correct. Eventually, Sam Costa sold his interest in his new claim for only five pounds. Sam's find turned out to be the richest part of the new gold field. He was a realist, however, and knew that he was unable to develop his claim. A new 'rush' began almost immediately after this sale of Costa's claim (Wilkinson, 1980).

Wilkinson (1980) has also suggested a good reason why the little gold township of Lunatic was so unusually named; she suggested that this name first belonged to a stallion called Lunatic. This stallion liked to escape from his paddock and to run off with some of the owner's mares. According to Wilkinson, he was invariably found in an open grassy area that was situated about six miles to the north of the homestead where he lived. This natural paddock was called Lunatic's paddock and when a gold and stibnite reef was discover there, the name of Lunatic was then adopted for the new town and gold reef (Wilkinson, 1980).

Future prospects for the old Tooloom goldfield:

The southern NEO was finished at the end of the Mesozoic Triassic but its legacy remains in its current and very complex landforms and, more importantly, in its extensive mineral deposits, much of which are reported to have been barely explored.

The story of the Phoenix Gold Project at Tooloom was included here in this story to illustrate the potential of this area for a future gold-mining revival at Tooloom. Recently, two Canadian Mining companies – Sentinel and RooGold, have been showing some interest in the general area with Sentinel acquiring a Gold Exploration Concession at South Tooloom in October 2020, while RooGold took up an Exploration Licence in the Peel Manning Suture Zone on the western side of the Clarence River in May 2022. Both those companies have been very focussed on finding new exploration areas with historical gold mines for both alluvial and reefal gold mining. Renewed interest in this old gold-mining area at Tooloom has thus now begun.

At the time of the gold rushes in 1859-62, it was not possible to give any clear explanation of why these 'golden gullies' of Tooloom had produced so much gold. Explanations began later after 1997 when Malachite Resources NL first began exploring these gullies but one gets the feeling whilst trying to fully account for the golden wealth of this region, that there is much still to learn about this fascinating but very complex tectonic region.

Road cutting near 'Lanaki' showing decomposing basalt
Source: Garry Gatfield, 2023

Milton panning for gold in the Clarence River catchment
Source: Garry Gatfield, 2024

14

Using local knowledge of ancient tracks to cross the Main Range

The colonial settlers were often assisted by local Indigenous peoples to find their way across an obstacle such as the Main Range at Toowoomba. Many of these new routes were simply the ancient tracks that the Indigenous people had used for many thousands of years to move around the region. A local tribal leader called 'King Multuggerah' from the Emu Creek and Helidon areas in the Lockyer Valley had, in the early 1840s, sent two of his sons and a number of warriors to show Lt. Gorman an easy passage to Drayton near Toowoomba from Helidon via One Tree Hill. This offer of help had unintended consequences some years later for both the Indigenous tribesmen and the colonial administrators in the Moreton Bay Penal Colony (Kerkhove, 2016).

The poisoning of Indigenous people near Tooloom on Kangaroo Creek Station by a local squatter:

In 1848, the manager of a sheep and cattle station named Kangaroo Creek in the Clarence area was charged with murdering eleven Indigenous persons by providing them with poisoned flour. After various run-ins with the local Indigenous population, the manager had invited several to his property to work for food. A servant testified that, at the end of the day, he had seen the manager provide the Indigenous men with a sack of what was presumed to be flour. The men had taken the flour back to their camp and made a damper. Days later, eleven bodies were discovered in a state of advanced decomposition by the Commissioner for Crown Lands in New South Wales - Mr Oliver Fry; he had visited the camp accompanied by the Police Constable and two officers after having received a complaint from locals. The remains of the poisoned damper was also discovered. As many as 23 Gumbaynggirr men may have been killed in this incident.

The station manager was duly apprehended and was charged with the crime. As the law stood at the time, however, Indigenous peoples could not give evidence in European courts and the presiding judge ordered that the station manager be immediately released due to a lack of evidence. In 1850, the manager sold the property and purchased Tooloom Station.

Incidents such as this and similar ones at Kilcoy Station and at Whiteside near Dayboro probably influenced the rebellion of the south-eastern Queensland Indigenous tribes in the 1840s. These Indigenous tribes met together every three years at the Bunya Nut Festival, which was held in the Bunya Mountains to the north of Toowoomba. Later, in 1875, a gentleman called Archibald Weston claimed to have recognised some of the Indigenous people from the Clarence and Richmond areas who were passing through the Lockyer Valley and were on their way to the Bunya Nut Festival.

An early check on the advance of the squatters into the Darling Downs region:

Our 'Special Correspondent' from the Moreton Bay Courier had decided to return to Brisbane from Tooloom via Warwick and this had necessitated a trip to Toowoomba and down the Main Range to Gatton. The staging post for dray traffic lay just to the south of Toowoomba on the Main Range at Drayton. The 'Special Correspondent' seemed strangely reluctant to describe this part of his journey in his letters from Tooloom, saying pointedly that:

It is not my intention to say anything of Drayton, as it has a local paper and local writers to advance the claims, which are not easily perceptible to the mere passers-by (Letters 9. 22nd of December, 1859).

Naturally, his reluctance to talk about Drayton piqued our author's interest and Garry's subsequent investigations turned up the dark and disturbing story of a rebellion that had taken place between a large number of Indigenous warriors from many tribes in Queensland's south-eastern region under the leadership of Old 'King Multuggerah' and the pastoralists or squatters. By the 1840s, these latter were now frequently travelling to Gatton from Moreton Bay and Ipswich and were then traversing up Gorman's Ridge to cross the Main Range at Drayton before moving beyond to the fertile Darling Downs and the grazing lands of the west.

The primary concern for the teamsters on the bullock drays passing through Drayton was, of course, the ease of access from Helidon up to Toowoomba. This route up Gorman's Ridge to the headwaters of Flagstone Creek took the bullock teams close to Mt Tabletop, which in those days was known as One Tree Hill.

This route to Drayton became known as Gorman's Gap after one such collaboration with the local Indigenous people. This collaboration started well but ended up very badly.

Old 'King Mutuggerah' was a powerful tribal headman in south-eastern Queensland, who had provided four Indigenous guides including two of his sons and, possibly, Moppy Multuggerah himself, to lead a group of white military explorers from the Moreton Bay Penal Settlement across the Main Range. These explorers were led by Lieutenant Gorman – the then Moreton Bay Commandant of the Moreton Bay Penal settlement, who was seeking an easier route to the Darling Downs. The route up Gorman's ridge was the same route taken by the tribesmen in their triennial trek to the Bunya Mountains Nut festival (Kerkhove, 2016 : 1).

Moppy Multuggerah - his son, was an Indigenous warrior and an inspired, resistance-leader, who was called variously 'King Multuggerah' and 'King Moppy'; he was born in 1820 and lived in the areas of Helidon, Lockyer and Emu Creeks and the Upper Brisbane River. Moppy Multuggerah is often confused with old 'King Multuggerah' in the retelling of their stories.

'King Multuggerah' first initiated hostilities against the Darling Downs' pastoralists in 1841 when a group led by him prevented pastoralist John Campbell and his flocks and bullocks from entering the Withcott area at the foot of the Main Range. Oral tradition has it that Campbell's men fled but John Campbell only escaped by kidnapping old 'King Multuggerah' himself. He met him again some weeks later and both greeted each other as friends. The first major aggression of Old 'King Multuggerah' took place only after the pastoralists began moving through the Main Range via Helidon; this took the form of an attack against Colinton Station near Esk where Old 'King Multuggerah' used 300 to 500 warriors to push Colinton's people and others off their runs. The pastoralist's overseer at Grantham then organised some raids of his own in which the eldest son of Old 'King Multuggerah's was killed (Kerkhove, 2016 : 7).

Old 'King Multuggerah' was now regarded as a serious threat by the pastoralists and, sometime later, he was shot dead whilst he was fishing by himself. His youngest son – Moppy Multuggerah (later King Moppy), was furious and vowed to take his vengeance on the pastoralists by running off their stock and by killing six white people (Kerkhov, 2016 : 7).

Runs were soon being attacked in earnest in the Lockyer Valley by Moppy Multuggerah's warriors and their stock scattered; these runs were soon, not only being damaged but were also being abandoned. A group of pastoralists met at Bonifant's Inn (in Gatton) and planned an offensive to retake and, to make safe, the passage up the ridge past Mt Tabletop (or One Tree Hill) to Drayton; their aim was to send much needed supplies to the new Darling Downs pastoral runs (Kerkhove, 2016 : 9).

On the13th of September 1843, Moppy Multuggerah's warriors successfully ambushed this dray train with its armed attendants of pastoralists and 30 to 45 of their servants as the drays were making their way up Gorman's Ridge past Mt Tabletop. This ambush forced the pastoralists and their servants to withdraw after an ensuing melee. Moppy Multuggerah and his warriors employed many clever strategies in this fight such as preventing the drays from backing out of the ambush by placing felled trees behind and in front of them; a copious supply of boulders were also rolled down from Mt Tabletop to injure the pastoralists and their servants and to smash their weapons (Kerkhove, 2016 : 4 -7).

No white persons were killed but casualties were much higher for the Indigenous warriors and at least one witness testified that he saw one warrior shot off Mt Tabletop (Helidon, Queensland Country Life 23 August 1900 p. 4). This was, indeed, a serious war that was being waged by Moppy Multuggerah and his warriors against the usurpers (Kerkhove, 2016 : 4 -5). Armed constables and mounted police came from as far away as Brisbane, Cressbrook and the Darling Downs (Kerkhove, 2016 p.8). This insurrection was treated very seriously by the Colonial Authorities in Brisbane and these built a small military fort in the Helidon area while military men were diverted to this fight to the detriment of the conduct of the Māori War then being fought in New Zealand (Kerkhove, 2016 p. 14).

Attacks against the pastoralists continued into 1846 and beyond. Eventually, Moppy Multuggerah and his hidden encampment in the Rosewood brigalow shrub were located by an Indigenous tracker and by a party of avenging settlers. In the ensuing battle in August 1846, Moppy Multuggerah and some of his group were killed in a dawn strike and, thereafter, Moppy Multuggerah's resistance war largely subsided, although some minor hostilities did persist for quite a number of years (Kerkhove, 2016 pp. 12 -15).

One of the most remarkable thing about Moppy Multuggerah's war is how this inspiring tribal leader could call on so many supporting warriors. Many have challenged this claim and denied his leadership feat but oral Indigenous tradition has it that he could call on in excess of 3,000 warriors and often used smoke signals to do so. In 1842, the new owner of the then Rosewood Station – Dr John Goodwin, claimed that he had found an Indigenous campsite on his property, where a count of the associated fireplaces suggested that Moppy Multuggerah had mustered around 1600 warriors at that very place (Kerkhove, 2016 pp.15-16).

The previously-mentioned triennial Bunya Festival was likely to have been one unique factor in the development of this Indigenous resistance; the Bunya Festival was normally a time for feasting, for meeting old friends, for holding coroborees and for sharing news and trade; inter-tribal marriages were also arranged at this time and the various tribal groups knew each other well. The 1840s was certainly the right time for a unifying leader to emerge out of these festivals. Kerkhove (2016 p.26) has also suggested that the Bunya Nut Festivals had made tribal warriors very familiar with the One Tree Hill route across the Main Range and that this familiarity then underpinned the planning of the resistance attacks on the pastoralists in the early 1840s (Kerkhove, 2016 pp. 19-20).

I also think that it was likely to have been significant that these resistance battles only happened after the pastoralist/squatters moved into the Helidon area. This was difficult country in which to fight a war. There were many rock shelters here with water sources and secret areas; this area would not only have given Multuggerah's tribe some protection from European raids but, having this would also have been a big source of self-confidence for them in organising their Indigenous resistance in the first instant.

The Sydney Morning Herald (12th of October 1843) showed Moppy Multuggerah little sympathy for his role as a resistance hero and observed that his attacks were:

unusually *daring.... (lasting) weeks... a regular systematic plan of plundering operations.*

Local journalists of the time were, however, far more generous in their assessment of Moppy Multuggerah with Duncan Cameron saying in the Warwick Examiner and Times (1915) that:

There was some spirit in the Moreton blacks, and it was their defence of One-Tree Hill in 1841 that gave the white man a respect for their fighting qualities.

James Porter, in the Darling Downs Gazette of the 21st of January 2011, also noted that the pastoralists had been humiliated at One Tree Hill by Moppy Multuggerah and his warriors:

It (the Battle) was a standing joke against the squatters that they allowed themselves to be worsted by the natives.

The pastoralists had never expected to lose, for these had previously focused on pre-emptive raids by armed men on horseback driving a big herd of cattle ahead of them to run off the existing

Indigenous tribesmen from their camps in the Darling Downs. This was quite effective as a strategy until they had moved on to Old Moppy Multuggerah's territory at Helidon below the Main Range at Toowoomba (Kerkhove, 2016 p.6).

William Wilkes, who was later to become the editor of the Moreton Bay Courier, even wrote a bush ballad called the 'The Raid of the Aborigines', which lampooned the squatters and appealed especially to the average Queenslander, for it humiliated the previously proud and mighty squatters in south-eastern Queensland. This song was known and sung for another eighty years (Kerkhove, 2016 : 2).

Moppy Multuggerah may have lost the final battle but the importance of his resistance was that it delayed settlement in the south-eastern region of Queensland for many years. Runs were abandoned for up to four to five years and the pastoralists of this region found it very hard to recover. Sporadic Indigenous attacks still occurred in this area for many years. (Kerkhove, 2016 : 24 and White and Kerkhove, 2016 p.7-10).

Would-be gold miners on the Tooloom goldfield certainly did not rush to use this alternative route to Ipswich from Tooloom via Warwick in and after, 1859.

Multuggerah's Way:

Multuggerah had probably been the Indigenous son of 'King Multuggerah' who had first led Lt Gorman over the Gorman's Ridge route in the early days of European settlement on the Darling Downs. He was also an inspiring resistance warrior who had fought tenaciously against the dispossession of his people from their traditional homelands and, in this role, he had shown tenacity, clever leadership and always, great courage.

These qualities and his leadership for his people have, thus, been recognised recently by the Toowoomba Regional Council. This body named the second road over the Toowoomba Range 'Multuggerah's Way' for this warrior on the 8thof September, 2019.

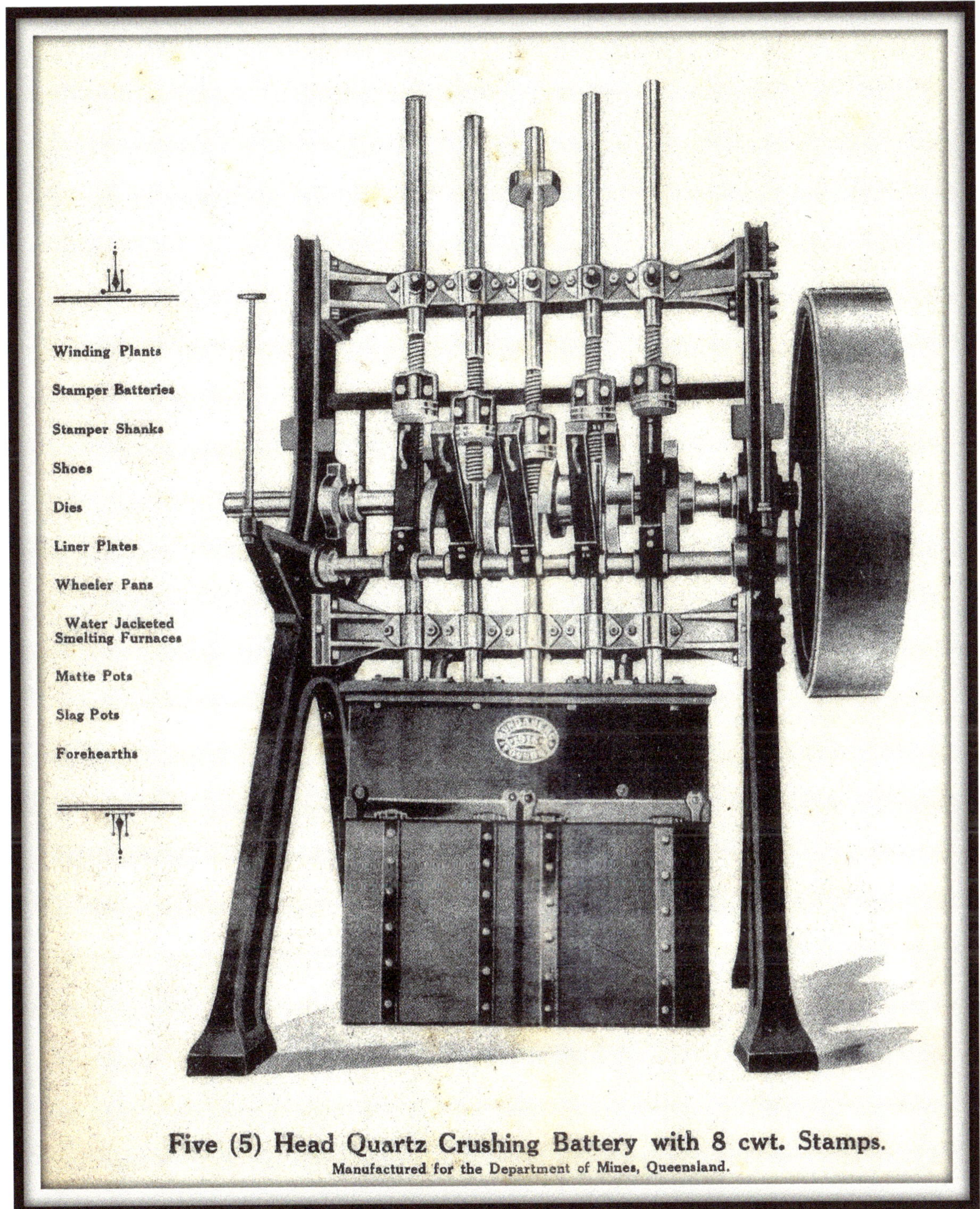

A typical 5 head stamper as used on the goldfields
Source: Old advertisement from a newspaper, via Trove, 2024

15

Conclusion: The effects of the gold rush on Australian society

A newly-arrived immigrant to New South Wales or Victoria in 1851 could easily have imagined themselves to be arriving in a penal colony. There were then around 400,000 non-indigenous persons in Australia at that time. Most of these were military persons, colonial administrators, convicts, 'ticket of leave' parolees' or squatters and their servants. Some merchants had also begun to open their own businesses and there was a growing new class of cedar-getters and ship-builders who were beginning to be noticed.

By 1861, the collected population of New South Wales, Queensland and Victoria had grown to 1.2 million; this rise in population was the direct result of the gold rushes in eastern Australia and, by 1878, Australia's population had risen further to 2.1 million. Most of this rise in population took place in Victoria and Melbourne was soon the second richest city in the British Empire after London. Most importantly, the bulk of these new arrivals were free settlers from different backgrounds and with diverse ideas about how they wanted to live.

As well as the broad sweep of English, Irish, Welsh and Scottish migrants, there was also a strong core of experienced Cornish miners. These were then followed by Germans, Scandinavians and by the American 'forty-niners' also with mining experience; these provided a ready pool of labour for the various trades and services in addition to the new mining-associated industries. New Zealanders also contributed to the gold rush as did the Chinese, whose arrival had pre-dated the start of the eastern Colonies gold rushes. The journey to our modern multi-cultural society had, thus, already begun. This influx of free-thinking immigrants has changed society from a feudal-like convict and penal settlement to a land of free settlers, farmers, tradesmen and labourers that not only included a new mercantile class, but also, a large number of dispossessed indigenous peoples.

With the gradual winning of a universal franchise in Australia after the 'Eureka Stockade Incident' in 1854, the power of the squatters was diminished as was Imperial rule from Great Britain. Previously, only land owners had been able to vote, which had effectively entrenched the power structure of the squatters and of the Governor and his administration. New wealth from gold had been able to break this nexus and the Eureka Incident had a major hand in this development for any man with a valid Miner's Right could then vote.

Gradually this voting right was extended to women with Australia and New Zealand leading the world on women's emancipation. Both countries had experienced substantial gold rushes – Australia in 1851 and New Zealand in 1861.

Of course, it was not all positive; there were at least three major negatives in the history of white settlement in Australia. The first was the dispossession of the Indigenous people, often by violent and deadly means; this remains an ugly blot on our history. The anti-Chinese sentiment on the goldfields eventually morphed into the official White Australia Policy and became law at the time of Federation in 1901, thus causing lasting bitterness for some worthy members of Australian society today; mutual Catholic/Protestant bigotry also poisoned Australian religious and societal attitudes until about the late 1960s. The repeal of the White Australia policy did not occur until more recent times but the resultant multicultural society that developed in the second half of the twentieth century has since enriched Australian society.

In the 1850s, the export of at least 85 % of the total output of gold from Australia led very quickly to gold surpassing wool as Australia's major export. The immense wealth so generated then contributed to a large number of different and positive outcomes as follows:

- Gold mining could support higher wages than could wool-based industries.
- Living standards rose and the working class grew to expect higher wages.
- Higher wages then encouraged the rise of trade unionism and gave some stability to local politics despite the ongoing inherent struggle between labour and capital.
- The lure of gold substantially increased immigration and population growth.
- Local manufacturing and industry were encouraged and those that were particularly focused on mining and allied services increased greatly.
- Gold mining gave rise to the notion and actual lived-experience of egalitarianism.
- The international economy relied on gold and supported the gold standard; the price of gold was fixed unlike wool, which could vary in times of drought and oversupply. This gave immense economic certainty to those employed in or investing in the gold-mining industry.
- As easy alluvial mining gave way to capital-intensive hard-rock mining, overseas capital flooded into Australia. This paved the way for social and political reform as well as for the direct development of the mining industry.
- The resultant economic boom allowed most Australians to enjoy one of the highest standards of living in the world.
- The wealth generated by gold mining allowed the colonies to finance significant areas of infrastructure such as the shipping ports, the extensive rail transport and the fine colonial government buildings.
- Regional towns sprang up adjacent to the new gold discoveries and those that survived contributed to the establishment of new service industries.
- Better government services such as law and order, education, hospitals, roads and bridges were able to be publicly provided.

- The development and growth of the local banking industry was largely facilitated by the needs of the gold rush.
- The local construction industry embarked on a period of grand building design and construction, the results of which still stand in former mining towns.
- The Australian mining industry is the largest contributor to Australia's export earnings today and our gold exports could soon see Australia overtake China as the world's leading producer.

I would be remiss not to mention the very important nation-building role of Cobb and Co during this long mining era in providing a superior and extensive network and mode of transport that was not only essential to Australia, from the 1850s to just after the first world war, but which we also exported to New Zealand and South Africa during their gold and diamond rushes.

The rise of large mining centres in Australia with expertise in extraction, processing and refining of ores, at places such as Broken Hill, Kalgoorlie and Mt Isa, which became world class.

The diggers from the goldfields and other mining centres became the nucleus of an Australian army that fought with distinction in both world wars.

There was a growing development of a new self-confidence in being Australian, especially in the rise of Australian poetry and art styles; this led to a feeling of nationhood and to the movement towards Australian Federation at the end of the 19th century.

Of the gold produced during the gold rush era, probably, less than 10% was retained within the country as currency (locally minted Gold Sovereigns), and as personal jewellery and specimens; the bulk was of course, exported to Great Britain, but some also ended up in China!

Some may claim that Australia was built on the 'sheeps back', but a more accurate assertion would be that 'Gold made Australia'.

Acknowledgements

All of the copious excerpts that I have quoted from the various newspapers were accessed via the *Trove* website. *Trove* is a portal into the collections of the National Library of Australia, which is a free service. Not only can you access digitised newspapers from 1803-1954 but you can correct mistakes in the transcriptions.

There is a wealth of information in it for the curious and for the keen historian of family history and local history. I have found Trove to be very useful for researching old goldfields and mineral deposits with a view to locating good and new fossicking spots.

I wish to acknowledge and thank Prof. Gideon Rosenbaum from the School of Earth and Environmental Sciences, Univ. of Qld. for his learned geological input and for his generous gift of much time for sharing his scientific knowledge of the geological development of the north-eastern New England Fold Belt with my contributing editor – Jane Eberhardt.

My appreciation is also extended to Prof. Peter Knights from the School of Mechanical and Mining Engineering, Univ. of Qld. for his generous foreword.

To my friend Jane Eberhardt, Editor and Contributing Author for this work, my gratitude is due for all your effort over the last few years - thank you.

To my daughter Cassandra Gatfield, I wish to thank her for extensive editorial assistance, without which, this would have been a very poor literary effort indeed.

To Cathy Ball - graphic artist, my sincerest appreciation for the cover design.

All photographs in this book were taken by this author and most maps and illustrations were, likewise, drafted by this author, except for those that are otherwise credited.

The *Special Correspondent,* writing for the *Moreton Bay Courier,* provided a wealth of useful knowledge with the narrative of his journey to Tooloom. I thought initially that *The Special Correspondent* may have been Fredrick Dalton – a reporter for the *SMH* but I am now convinced that he was most likely to have been Frederick Sinnett - a reporter for the Melbourne *Argus.* I have deduced this and the author of '*The Rockhampton Delusion*' - Lorna McDonald, has also identified him as the *Argus* correspondent who wrote extensively on the Canoona rush. He also republished his *Argus* articles as an 1859 book - *'Rush to Port Curtis'*, under his own name. He died very young at the age of 36; this was probably from hardship and disease suffered on his many rough journeys, when reporting on gold rushes in NSW, VIC, and QLD. We also know that our *Special Correspondent* was at the Canoona rush prior to his arrival in Moreton Bay and that he then attended the Tooloom rush, because he tells us so.

My gratitude also goes to the many long-deceased, other journalists and contributors from the various newspapers that I have quoted from.

I acknowledge that Isabel Wilkinson started this journey for me when she wrote *'Forgotten Country'* in 1980. We have now continued her story of the Upper Clarence goldfields. There is certainly a wealth of history of this area still to be uncovered!

Christopher Dawson from the Boggo Road Gaol Historical Society published a book in 2010, which had consisted of nine letters by *The Special Correspondent -A Trip to the Diggings.* His publication predates this effort by 14 years but I must also mention that I had independently discovered the writings of The *Special Correspondent'* at around that same time in Trove.

Brett J. Stubbs published '*The Gold Digger's Arms, Pubs of the Upper Clarence River district, New South Wales'* in 2009 *and, w*hilst mainly concerned with hotels, he covered some of the early history of the Tooloom Diggings. He appears to concur with my assessment of Perkins' discovery of gold at Tooloom.

For the use of the opening scene – a watercolour of Tooloom painted in October 1860 by Conrad Wagner, I gratefully acknowledge the Mitchell Library from the State Library of NSW, which had only recently purchased this historic work at auction in 2017. It is the only known view of Tooloom in the early Gold Rush era, that I am aware of.

Original spelling in my source materials has mostly been retained but, in some instances, the modern or corrected spelling has been used instead or has been added in brackets for clarification and for ease of reading.

Finally, I wish to acknowledge my cousin, Milton, for all those wonderful fossicking trips that we have enjoyed together (over 300), including many to Tooloom.

Historic Errors

Various claims have been made that the discovery of gold at Tooloom was made by Billy May. All research instead points to James Perkins and Party as the legitimate claimants. Another claim by Big Joe - the Californian miner, that he discovered Tooloom was dismissed as well, as you have seen. At least one other party also tried to claim the glory of the discovery; their claim was similarly discounted.

Others have written that the locality of the discovery of '*The Lady Bowen Nugget*' has been lost and is, consequently, unknown; that is also false as I have demonstrated. Earlier dates have been claimed for the original gold discovery at Tooloom, some as early as 1857. This assertion has now been clearly disproved. The number of diggers on the whole of the Tooloom goldfield at its peak was probably around 2,000; some have claimed 10,000, which is a totally unsupported number!

Just prior to publication, my research revealed an obituary for William May in 1907.

The following article inferred that he may have been one of the un-named members of Perkins' party. There are also, however, a few problems with this story! The original discovery became known as Upper Tooloom, not Lower Tooloom. The Lower Tooloom Diggings were later discovered downstream. The reward claim (the extra ground on Tooloom Creek that was awarded to the discoverer) did not pay well at all. Perkins and Party later pegged a reward claim in Joe's Gully that paid handsomely; Joe's Gully is reputed to have produced over a ton of gold. The article below also infers that their claim covered most of Joe's Gully and that May and his mates got most of the gold. This was definitely not the case. Should we trust this story with three such obvious errors? This story was also written nearly 50 years after the event (in *The Tenterfield Intercolonial Courier & Fairfield & Wallangarra Advocate* 16 July 1907).

> *DEATH OF AN OLD COLONIST. - A correspondent reports the death on the 30th. June last, of one of Tooloom's oldest residents in the person of William May, who was born in Sussex a few days after the eventful 18th of June 1815 (the Battle of Waterloo). He came to N. S. Wales in the early fifties as a petty officer on the old steamer "Grafton," under Captain Wiseman. After running a few months with his old captain between Sydney and Grafton, he, like many of his time, drifted to the gold mines near Armidale.*
>
> *He proceeded from thence to Timbarra and, with others,* (possibly Perkins and Party), *went on a prospecting tour towards what is now the north boundary of the colony; on their return, they found the Lower Tooloom goldfield where they were granted a large prospecting claim of*

exceedingly rich ground. It was worked for many years and over a ton of gold came out of it as a result of their labour but, like the ways of many more of the miners of those days, the money went as quickly as it was so easily got. The latter years of Mr. May's life, although in poor circumstances, were passed in comfort. There were few who had a hard word to say of old 'Billy,' and now, after fifty years residence in the district, he has gone where there is no more labour.

Further research revealed this second obituary but it makes no mention of him being the original discoverer of the Tooloom goldfield and that he was merely a successful long-term digger at Tooloom.

Richmond River Express and Casino Kyogle Advertiser 9 July 1907.

Tooloom.

Again, I have to chronicle the death of a pioneer named William May who breathed his last on Sunday week, at the age of 92 years. He was a native of Sussex and came to this country about 63 years ago. In 1856-7, he was a steward on board the old Grafton under Captain Wiseman who was then running on the Clarence River.

In '58, he came to the Tooloom diggings to seek his fortune with the big crowd that had come from Grafton, McLeod's Creek, and other places too numerous to mention, wherever the news of the new find had spread. He was very successful and at one time held the richest claim that was on Tooloom; it is stated from persons who should know, that he got more gold than any other man on the diggings.

He was very liberal and his purse was ever open to any old mates who were not as successful as himself. He was very much liked in and around the district and the large crowd of people who attended his funeral on July 1st gave ample proof that he was held in the highest esteem by the residents of the Tooloom diggings. From the year '58 to the present time, he has never been out of the district.

In later years, things were not so brilliant with him and when the old-age pension came into force, he was obliged to apply for it. On this, he has been able to live free from want. About two years ago, he was taken ill and was unable to help himself. Mr. Kenneth McLean and his good wife had kindly brought him to their home at Kangaroo Flat, where, he became strong under their care and was soon able to get about as usual.

About five weeks ago he had an attack of paralysis and, from then, never left his bed. He became as helpless as a child and after terrible suffering passed over on Sunday week.

The funeral arrangements were creditably carried out by Mr. C. Mealing, of Tooloom.

William May can't have arrived at Tooloom Diggings in 1858, they weren't discovered until April 1859, but if he was one of Perkins' Party who worked the Timbarra or Tableland Diggings in 1858 and then subsequently went prospecting in early 1859 with Perkins and discovered Tooloom, that is a more likely sequence of events.

Timeline for the 'Lady Bowen Nugget'

Wed. 7. December 1859

Thu. 8. 1pm, Mr. Ogilvie departed the Diggings, (a nugget was found 1 hour prior to his departure).

Fri. 9. Ogilvie arrived at Ipswich in the evening after a hard, two-day horse-ride.

Sat. 10. The story was penned as a news article heading on Saturday evening.

Sun. 11.

Mon. 12.

Tue. 13. The *North Australian* was the first newspaper to mention the nugget discovery.

Wed. 14.

Thu. 15. A detailed article was published by the *Moreton Bay Courier* announcing the discovery.

Fri. 16.

Sat. 17.

Sun. 18.

Mon. 19. The gold escort departed Tooloom with 345 ozs of gold including the nugget.

Tue. 20.

Wed. 21. The gold escort arrived in Ipswich with the nugget and Templeton, on the same day that the Governor and Lady Bowen arrived for their first official visit. They viewed the nugget.

Thu. 22. The nugget arrived in Brisbane and a full description was printed.

From the above timeline, we can logically deduce that the 'Lady Bowen Nugget' was discovered around 12 noon on the 8th of December, 1859. Presumedly on Saturday the 10th, after he had rested from his ride, Ogilvie related the news to the reporter who wrote the article that evening. It wasn't, however, published until Thursday the 15th - a week after the event. One newspaper article reported the actual time of discovery was 11am.

Relevant excerpt from the main newspaper that announced the discovery:

The Moreton Bay Courier (15 Dec. 1859). IPSWICH.

(From our own correspondent.)

Saturday evening.

Mr Ogilvy returned yesterday evening from the diggings, having left at 1 p.m. on Thursday last. About an hour before he left a nugget of pure gold was found, weighing 140 ozs. 15 dwts.

Clarence River Goldfields and Mineral Localities

Gold Locality	Discovered	By Whom
Boonoo Boonoo.	Dec 1857.	G.T. Maxwell
Boorook	Early 1871	
Bulldog Diggings.	861	
Cangi.	1861?	
Doctors Gully		
Drake (Fairfield).	Jan 1886?	
Dry Gully.	1859	
Eight Mile.	Late1859	
Emu Creek.	Mid 1859	
Ewingar Creek.	1861	
Fays Gully.	1859	
Frasers Creek.	1859/60?	
Joe's Gully.	1859	
Long Gully	1858/9?	
Lunatic.	1869?	
Malara Creek.	1858/9?	
Marylands River.	Oct 1859	
McLean's Creek		
McLeod's Creek.	1858	
Millera Creek		
Mosquito Creek.	July 1859	
Nelsons Creek.	1858/9?	
Nicholson's Creek.	1861?	
Paddy's Flat		
Poverty Point.	1858/9?	
Pretty Gully.	Oct 1859?	
Red Rock.	1887?	
Rivertree (Silver).	1888?	
Sandy Creek.	1858?	
Surface Hill.	1858?	
Timbarra Tablel.	1858?	
Timbarra River	Oct 1857?	

Tooloom Creek.	April 1859	Perkins and Party
White Rock (Silver)	1887	John Rossiter

This list is not exhaustive.

It should be noted that I haven't fully researched or documented the discovery of all these individual goldfields or localities. That is for another time or person.

A question mark after the date indicates only 1 source (in Trove) has been consulted, so the discovery date is still unconfirmed; until additional sources have been found.

Currency, Weights and Distance

The imperial system of money and weights is confusing for many, especially for those in the modern metric era.

Why does d. mean penny? as in pennyweight, and why is cwt. a hundredweight?

We owe these terms to the Latin language of the Romans. In Roman numerals **c** represents 100 and this explains the cwt.

The denarius was a Roman coin that gave us the legacy of 'd.' as the abbreviation for the English penny. Similarly, the Roman coin - the solidus gave us the abbreviation for the shilling - 's.', and, finally, the pound symbol - £ derives from the Roman word Librae denoting, when originally brought to Britain, a pound in weight of gold or silver – thus £-s-d. (Pound-shilling-pence).

For over 500 years, gold has primarily been weighed and sold legally in Troy weight. Consequently, 1oz of gold is equal to 31.1grams, **not** 28.35grams; that is an avoirdupois oz.

It is basically fraud to sell an ounce of gold weighed as avoirdupois, because the seller is attempting to defraud the buyer of nearly 3 grams (42.5 grains) of gold!

Most modern digital scales can weigh accurately in troy, as well as carats (for gemstones), metric grams, and avoirdupois. Beam-balance scales as sold by gun-shops for weighing powder, use the imperial grain and so are also suitable for weighing gold.

The distance from Ipswich to Tooloom was roughly 80 miles, so this was about 130km - a 2-day ride by horse. Tooloom was less than 20 miles direct from the new border, so it was about 30km.

1 mile=1.61 km

1 km=0.62 mile

In keeping with the theme of this narrative, I have not converted any of the Imperial weights and measures from the gold rush era to metric. I remind readers that the universal price of gold is still officially quoted in US Dollars per 1 troy ounce.

Current TV programs concerning gold mining use a mixture of weights – (usually grams) for pieces below an ounce in weight, then revert to troy ounces for nuggets above an ounce – a nonsensical situation!

Anyone who enters the gold business quickly realises that they must know the troy weight system. It is easy if you remember the Imperial grain is the basic unit for all three of the Imperial weight systems, and is the same in all three.

Starting with 1 grain, if we have 24, then that equals 1 pennyweight (dwt), so a nice little 1 dwt nugget is about 1.5 grams. There are 20dwts in 1 troy ounce (oz), currently valued in Australia at about $3,100, (Dec. 2023). Simple!

Troy

24 grains (gr) = 1 pennyweight (dwt)

20 dwt = 1 ounce (oz)

12 oz. = 1 pound (lb) (The UK abolished the Troy Pound as a legal weight in 1879).

480 gr = 1 oz

5,760 gr = 1 lb

Old weight chart

(out of copyright)

Avoirdupois

27.34375 gr = 1 dram

16 drams = 1 oz

437.5 gr = 1 oz

16 ozs = 1 lb

7,000 gr = 1 lb

14 lb = 1 stone

28 lb = 1 quarter (qr)

4 qr = 1 hundredweight (cwt)

112 lb = 1 cwt

20 cwt = 1 ton

2,240 lb = 1 ton

Apothecaries

20 gr = 1 scruple

3 scruples = 1 drachm

8 drachm = 1 oz

1 oz apoth = 1 oz troy

The Grain

1 troy gr = 1 apoth gr = 1 avoir gr

1 gr = 0.0648 metric grams = 64.8 milligrams

Metric

1000 milligrams = 1 gram (g)

1000 g = 1 kilogram (kg)

1000 kg = 1 tonne - metric ton

1 g = 15.432 grains

Ounce (oz)

1 troy oz = 480 gr

1 avoir. oz = 437.5 gr

1 apoth. oz = 480 gr

1 troy oz = 31.1035 g

1 avoir. oz = 28.35 g

Carat (ct)

1 ct = 3.17 grains (prior to the metric standard, 1903) Old

1 ct = 3.0865 grains (after 1903) Modern

1 ct = 0.2 grams (Ditto) Modern

1 gram = 5 cts

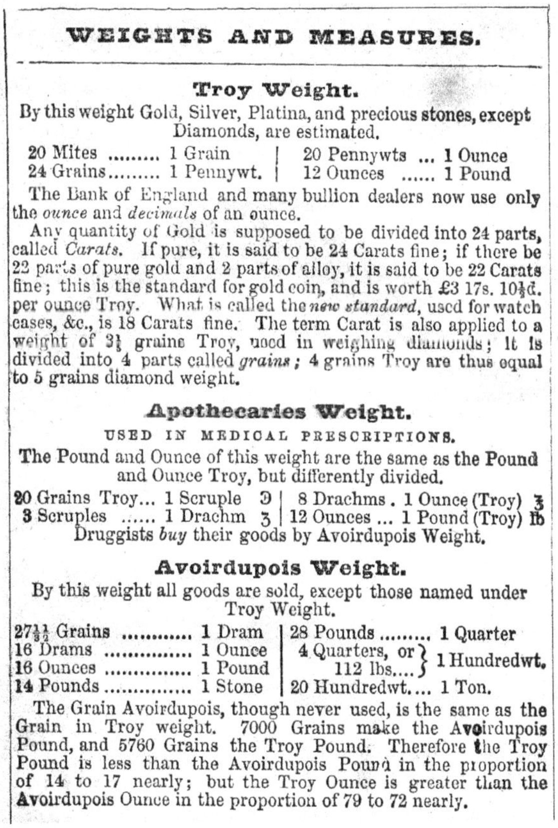

WEIGHTS AND MEASURES.

Troy Weight.

By this weight Gold, Silver, Platina, and precious stones, except Diamonds, are estimated.

20 Mites	1 Grain	20 Pennywts ...	1 Ounce
24 Grains.........	1 Pennywt.	12 Ounces	1 Pound

The Bank of England and many bullion dealers now use only the *ounce* and *decimals* of an ounce.

Any quantity of Gold is supposed to be divided into 24 parts, called *Carats*. If pure, it is said to be 24 Carats fine; if there be 22 parts of pure gold and 2 parts of alloy, it is said to be 22 Carats fine; this is the standard for gold coin, and is worth £3 17s. 10½d. per ounce Troy. What is called the *new standard*, used for watch cases, &c., is 18 Carats fine. The term Carat is also applied to a weight of 3⅕ grains Troy, used in weighing diamonds; it is divided into 4 parts called *grains*; 4 grains Troy are thus equal to 5 grains diamond weight.

Apothecaries Weight.

USED IN MEDICAL PRESCRIPTIONS.

The Pound and Ounce of this weight are the same as the Pound and Ounce Troy, but differently divided.

20 Grains Troy...	1 Scruple ℈	8 Drachms .	1 Ounce (Troy) ℥
3 Scruples	1 Drachm ʒ	12 Ounces ...	1 Pound (Troy) ℔

Druggists *buy* their goods by Avoirdupois Weight.

Avoirdupois Weight.

By this weight all goods are sold, except those named under Troy Weight.

27 11/32 Grains	1 Dram	28 Pounds	1 Quarter
16 Drams	1 Ounce	4 Quarters, or 112 lbs....	1 Hundredwt.
16 Ounces	1 Pound	20 Hundredwt....	1 Ton.
14 Pounds	1 Stone		

The Grain Avoirdupois, though never used, is the same as the Grain in Troy weight. 7000 Grains make the Avoirdupois Pound, and 5760 Grains the Troy Pound. Therefore the Troy Pound is less than the Avoirdupois Pound in the proportion of 14 to 17 nearly; but the Troy Ounce is greater than the Avoirdupois Ounce in the proportion of 79 to 72 nearly.

Old Weight Chart

Source: via Trove, out of copyright

List of Tooloom Signatories December 1860

TO G.W.F. ADDISON, Esq, Gold Commissioner,

Tooloom - Sir, - We, the undersigned publicans, storekeepers, miners, and others resident on Upper, Lower, Tooloom, and Pretty Gully, beg to record our unqualified approbation at the pleasing and satisfactory manner in which you have discharged your duties as commissioner and magistrate during your residence on these gold-fields. We also attribute to your intelligence and activity, the general peace and good order we enjoy. It is, moreover, our opinion that all cases of dispute and adjudication have been most satisfactorily disposed of, through the kind and gentlemanly conduct which has at all times characterised your intercourse with the resident population.

In conclusion, we beg to offer our warmest wishes for your future welfare, and express our hope that your stay amongst us may be long continued, and our interests correspondingly advanced.

We are, Sir, your obedient servants,

John Drysdale, storekeeper. Peter Farrell, miner. John Camron, miner.
Richard Gwatkin, miner. John Whyford, miner. Robert Clarke, miner.
Martin Anderson, miner. Joseph Stephens, miner. Walter Eden, miner.
William Summer, miner. Samuel Lee, miner. Donald McDougall, miner.
Francis James, miner. James Robinson, miner. Henry Maurice, miner.
William Schultz, miner. John Melville, miner. Edward Hannan, miner.
James Brown, miner. James Wakelin, miner. Edward Low, miner.
Nicol B Stirrat miner. Henry Watson, miner. James Tiernan, miner.
John Williams, miner. E. Young, miner. O. Sykes.
Michael Kenny, miner. John Randall, miner. John Fraser, miner.
E. P. Betts, storekeeper. J. D. Webster, miner. Frederick Coleman, miner.
Peter Maine, miner. Anthony Sullivan, miner. John Martin, miner.
Walter Black, innkeeper. Henry Douling, miner. W.P. Dowling, miner.
G. E. Cole, overseer, Woodenberry William Williams, miner.
Thomas Binitt, butcher.
Edward Sharpe, miner. John Lowrie, miner. William McKay, miner.
John Smith, miner. James Scrase, miner. George Green, miner.
Charles Korjorn, miner. Joseph Walker, miner. **W. May, miner.**
William Wilson, miner. J. Roberts, miner. Thos. Akin, bullock driver.

Martin, miner. Edward Humphries, miner. Henry Sidewell, miner.
James Mitchell, miner. Florence Carey, miner. Edward Santer, miner.
Joseph Bailey, miner. Edward Pertrale, miner. John Irwin, miner.
John Brown, miner. Thomas Condon, miner. Anne Cooke, publican.
Farquhar McRae, miner. John Williams, miner. Thomas Wardlow.
John Mills, miner. James Jennings, miner. Edward Helden, publican.
James Hornes, miner. Nat Neegan, miner. James Smith, miner.
Tererence Gorman, miner. J. Duncan, junior, butcher. John W. Wilson, miner.
Robert Gordon, butcher. John Cross, miner. John Dunbar Grant, miner.
Donald McLean, storekeeper. Edward Richards, miner. **James S. Perkins, miner.**
D. McLean, Junior, storekeeper. John McLean, storekeeper. William Huggings, miner.
John McKay, storekeeper. Robert Grant, miner. James Rands, storekeeper.
Wm. Higgings, junior, miner. Rodrick Cameron, storekeeper. Henry Steiden, shoemaker.
Henry Smith, miner. Samuel Avery, miner. John Martin, miner.
Daniel Tynan, miner. Thomas Lane, miner. John McPhee, miner.
John Mahony, miner. John McPhee, miner. Jeremiah Smith, miner.
James Comes, miner. Henry Brimmer, blacksmith. J. W. Sandford, miner.
William Fitch, storekeeper. Thomas Barren, miner. John Galigan, miner.
James Doyle, miner. George Ewen, miner. Robert King, miner.
Cornelius Lane, miner. A. McKinny, miner. William Wilson, miner.
John Peterson, miner. William Jones, miner. William Young, miner.
John Monks, miner. Duncan McIntyre, miner. David McLean, storekeeper.
Alexander Gruer, miner. Finly McGuire, miner. B. M. Turner, miner.
Kenuth McClure, miner. Robert Davidson, Innkeeper. John Aitken, miner.
George Hiron, storekeeper. F. J. Lack, superintendent Tooloom Station.
P. Hanson, miner. William Thomas, miner. William O'Donnell, miner.
Dick Mattock, miner. George Aitken, postmaster. John Beresford, miner.
John McCreay, miner. Thomas Parker, miner. John Brock, publican.
G. W. Wilmoth, miner. Thos. Aitken, storekeeper. James Irvine, miner.
Gordon Cameron, storekeeper, Lower Tooloom. William McDonald, miner.
S. C. Pollard, miner. Daniel McFarlane, butcher. Edward Keeffe, miner.
Richard Saunders, miner. Ralph Eldridge, miner. John Ike, miner.
Frank Stein, miner. F. Atkinson, miner. John Wilson, miner.
Mr. G Finch, miner. John Williams, miner. Walter Kemp, miner.
Paul Holloway, miner. D. D. McCarthy, miner. **John Farley, miner.**
Samuel Wilson, miner. Edward Smith, miner. W. W. Langley, miner.
James McKierchan, miner. John Cooper, miner. George Hampson, miner.

Perkins and May are discussed elsewhere, but John Farley had a long association with the nearby Pretty Gully Goldfield as publican, storekeeper and miner.

Tooloom Creek Gold Field Map 1936

Acknowledgement: The cropped map image of 'The Tooloom Creek Gold Field' on the following page is included courtesy of the National Library of Australia.

This edition of the map was originally published in 1936 by the Department of Lands, Sydney, NSW, also acknowledged.

The dark line following the Eastern boundary of Tooloom Creek was an addition to the map in 1971, depicting the Kyogle Shire boundary.

Map of the County of Buller, Eastern Division, N.S.W.
Date : 19/02/22 4:26 PM
https://nla.gov.au:443/tarkine/nla.obj-564498983
Edition Out of Copyright
Reason for copyright status: Since 1961
Copyright status was determined using the following information:
Material type: Artistic
Published status: Published
Publication date: 1971

The main alluvial gold bearing area extends from Slaughteryard Creek (Gully), located just above the township reserve, to Darke's Point where Tooloom Creek joins the Clarence River. Joe's Gully and Peg Leg Gully are located on the western-side of Tooloom Creek. Lower Tooloom and Humbug Gully are marked on the east-bank, further south.

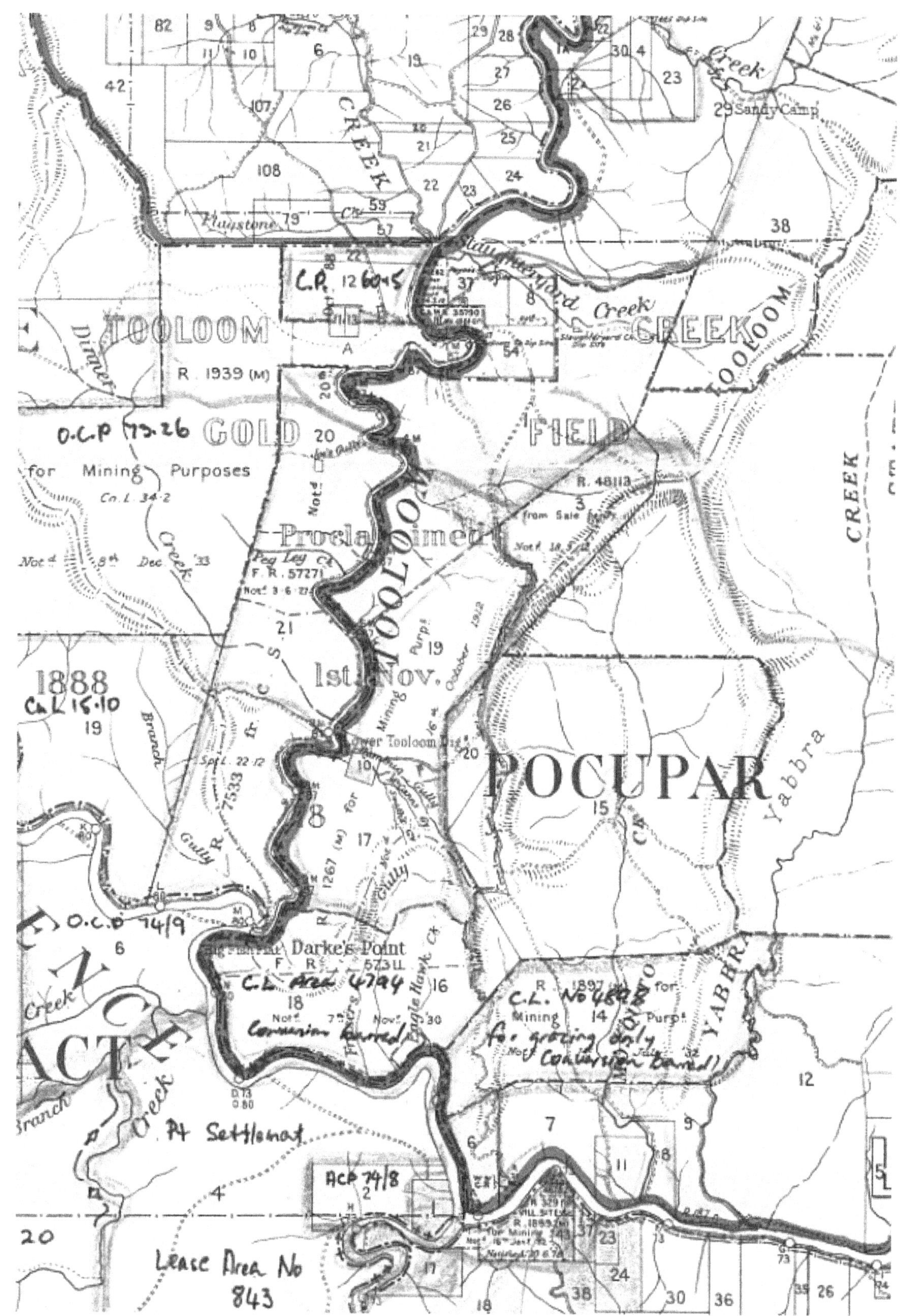

Tooloom Creek Gold Field Map
Source: Dept of Lands, Sydney, 1936, out of Copyright via Trove

Bibliography I. A social history of the Eastern Australian goldfields

1. Carrington, D.L. (1960). The Gold Rushes of New South Wales – 1851-74: A Social History. Thesis. Aust. Nat. Univ. Canberra. 281pp. openresearch-repository.anu.edu.au.
2. Crowley, F.K. (1980). Timeline - The Australian Gold Rush. Nelson, 1980.
3. Goodwin, T. (2018). *Gold's influence on Australia's Economic Development in the 19th Century.* The ANU Undergraduate Research Journal. Vol 9. 10pp.
4. Nelson (1980). *The Australian gold rushes.* In A Documentary History of Australia, Vol 2 Colonial Australia 1841- 1874. Nelson.
5. *Attacking the Mail, Bush-ranging NSW 1864.* TLF Resource R3383. Education Services and National Library of Australia. (2013).
6. Hamilton, J.P. QC. (2014). Adjudication on the goldfields of New South Wales and Victoria in the 19th century. Macquarie Law School Faculty of Arts. Macquarie Univ. 417pp.
7. Jones, F. (2000). *Forbes to Orange Escort Robbery at Eugowra.* New South Wales Dept. of Primary Industries (replaces Minfact 93).
8. Kerkhove, R. (2016). Multuggerah and Multuggerah Way. https://www.academia.edu>multuggerah_and_multuggerah_way 39pp.
9. Mahar, C. Gold – Concept. Commissioners: A History of Criminal Law in New South Wales. Viewed online at Heritage Victoria.
10. Serle, G. (1963). The golden age: A History of the Colony of Victoria 1851-1861. Melbourne University Press, Melbourne, Victoria.
11. Stubbs, B. J. (2007). A Thematic History of the City of Grafton. Community-based Heritage Project. Vol 2. NSW heritage Office and Clarence Valley Council.111pp
12. *The Gold Commissioners of New South Wales.* From eGold – A Nation's Heritage. egold.net.au/biogs?EG00182b.htm.
13. The State of Queensland. (2001). Redefining the Queensland-New South Wales Border Guidelines for Surveyors. Dept. Nat, Res. and Mines. Qld. https://www.resources.qld.gov.au › assets>pdf>file). 33pp.
14. Ward, J.M. (1966). *Fitzroy, Sir Charles Augustus (1796-1858),* Australian Dictionary of Biography, Australian National University. 8 pp.

1. White, S and R. Kerkhove. (2021). *Indigenous laws of war: Makarrata, Milwerangel and Junkarti.* In International Committee of the Red Cross, ICRC. No.914 at international-review.icrc.org/articles/indigenous-australian-laws-of-war. pp.20.
15. Wilkinson, I. (1980). Forgotten Country: The Story of the Upper Clarence Gold Fields. Northern Rivers College of Advanced Education. 291pp.
16. Smith, G. (1926). *A contribution to the Mineralogy of New South Wales, Mineral Resources No. 34,* NSW Department of Mines.

Bibliography II. Geology of the North-eastern New England Fold Belt and Tooloom

1. Aitcheson, J.C. and Flood, P.G. (1993). *Gamilaroi Terrane: A Devonian rifted intra-oceanic island arc assemblage.* Dept. Geology and Geophysics. Univ. of Sydney, 2006. Australia and Dept Geology and Geophysics. Univ. of New England. NSW. 2351, Australia.
2. Ball, P. W., Czarnota, K., White, N. J., Klöcking, M., and Davies, D. R. (2021). *Thermal structure of eastern Australia's upper mantle and its relationship to Cenozoic volcanic activity and dynamic topography.*in Geochemistry, Geophysics, Geosystems, 22, e2021GC009717. 22pp.
3. Beeson, R. and D. Borten. (2015). *The Mt. Carrington Epithermal Gold-Silver-Zinc System and the Host Drake Volcanics.* at https://smrdg,org,au>uploads>2015/05 6pp.
4. Blevin, P.L.(2010). *Igneous metallogenic contrasts between the northern and southern New England Orogen, Eastern Australia,* in NEO 2010: Conf. Proceedings. School of Earth and Environmental Earth Sciences. Univ. of Wollongong. New South Wales. pp. 40-44.
5. Blevin, P. L. (2010). *Old friends in a whole new light: A new chronology for the igneous metallogeny of the southern New England Orogen, New South Wales.* In NEO 2010: Conf. Proceedings. School of Earth and Environmental Earth Sciences. Univ. of Wollongong. New South Wales. pp. 45-48.
6. Buckman, S. and P. Blevin. (2010). *The New England Orogen,* in Preface to NEO 2010: Conf. Proceedings. School of Earth and Environmental Earth Sciences. Univ. of Wollongong. New South Wales. pp ix – xv.
7. Buckman, S., Line, T., Aitchison and A. Nutman. (2010). *Cu mineralisation with intrusive phases of the Gamilaroi and Weraerai terranes at Barry Station, southern New England Orogen.* Conf. Proc. School of Earth and Environmental Earth Sciences. Univ. of Wollongong. New South Wales. pp. 87-93.
8. Chappell, B. W., Bryant, C. J. and D. Wyborn. (2012). *Peraluminous I-Type Granite* in Lithos. 153 pp. pp142-153.
9. Coenraads, R. R., Ollier, C.D. (1992). *Tectonics and Landforms of the New England Region Field Conference - New England District.* Geological Society of Australia Queensland Division. 54pp.
10. Cohen, R. and R. C. Dunlop. (2004). *Timbarra Gold Deposit: New England Region, New South Wales.* School of Biological, Earth and Environmental Sciences, Univ. of New South Wales. 3pp.

11. Ealing-Godbold, C. (2014). Senior Librarian, Information Services. *The Great 'Tin rush' of Stanthorpe.'* State Library of Queensland.
12. Ferguson, C. L (2019). *Subduction, accretion and orocline development in modern and ancient settings: Implications of Japanese examples for the development of the New England Orogen of Eastern Australia.* Journal of Geodynamics 129. School of Earth and Environmental Sciences. Univ. of Wollongong, NSW. pp. 117-130.
13. Flood, P.G. and Aitcheson, J.C. (1993). *Recent advances in understanding the geological development of the New England province of the New England Orogen.* In NEO '93 Conf. Proceed. (1993). Univ. of New England, Armidale. pp. 61-67.
14. Ford, A., Peters, K.J., Partington, G.A., Blevin, P.L., Downes, P.M., Fitzherbert, J.A., and Greenfield, J.E. (2019). *Translating expressions of intrusion-related mineral systems into mappable spatial proxies for mineral potential mapping: Case studies from the Southern New England Orogen, Australia.* In Ore Geology Reviews Vol 111. Aug 2019, 102943.
15. Geociences Australia (2023). *Minerals.* In Earth Sciences for Australia's Future. Geoscience Australia.
16. Glen, R.A. (2013). *The Tasminides of Eastern Australia.* Geological Survey of New South Wales. Dept. Primary Industries. P.O Box 344. Hunter Region Mail Centre. NSW. 2319, 74pp.
17. Glen, R.A., and Scheibner, E. (1993). *Lachlan rocks in the New England Orogen* in NEO '93 Conf. Proc. (1993). Geological Survey of NSW. Depart. Mineral Resources, St Leonards, NSW. pp. 123-126.
18. Groves D. I, Goldfarb R. J, Gebre-Mariam M, Hagemann S.G, and Robert F (1998). *Orogenic gold deposits: a proposed classification in the context of their crustal distribution and relationship to other gold deposit types.* Ore Geol. Rev. 13: pp. 7-27.
19. Groves, D. I (2019). *Orogenic gold deposits: part of a global dynamic conjunction between subduction and gold.* Orebusters Pty Ltd. 7 Kellett Close, Gwelup, WA.
20. Henderson, R.L., C.L. Ferguson., E.C. Leitch., V. J. Morand., J.J.Reinhardt and P.F. Carr. (1993). *Tectonics of the Northern New England Fold Belt.* In NEO '93 Conf. Proceed. (1993). Univ. of New England, Armidale (322419378).
21. Hoy, D., Rosenbaum, G., Wormald, R., and U. Shaanan. (2014). *Geology and Geochronology of the Emu Creek Block (Northern New South Wales, Australia) and Implications for oroclinal bending in the New England Orogen.* In Australian Journal of Earth Sciences. Geological Society of Australia. 61. pp.1109-1124.
22. Jessop, K., Daczko, N.R. and Piazolo, S. (2018). *The Tectonic Cycles of the New England Orogen of Eastern Australia.* Australian Research Council Centre of Excellence for Core to Crust Fluid Systems (CCFS) and GEMOC, Department of Earth and Planetary Sciences, Macquarie University, NSW. Australia and School of Earth and Environment, Faculty of Environment, Univ. of Leeds, LS2 9JT UK.

23. Lawrie, K. C., Chan, R.A., Gibson, D., and Kovacs, N. (1999). *Alluvial gold potential in buried paleochannels in the Wyalong district, Lachlan Fold Belt, New South Wales.* In AGSO Research Newsletter 30. 5pp.
24. Laukamp, C. (2013). *Fault Lines lead to Gold.* Curtain University – ARC Centre of Excellence for Core to Crust Fluid Systems and CSIRO Report. Ore Geology Reviews. @https://www.csiro.au/en/news/all/articles/2013/june/fault-lines-lead-to-gold
25. Li, P-f., Rosenbaum, G., and Vasconcelos, P. (2014). *Chronological restraints on the Permian geodynamic evolution of Eastern Australia.* Journal of Tectonophysics. 617. School of Earth Sciences, Univ. of Queensland, St Lucia. Brisbane. Australia. pp.11.
26. Line, T.W. (2011). *Shrimp Geochronology of the southern New England Orogen.* B. of Sc. (Honours). School of Earth and Envoirnmental Sciences, Univ. of Wollongong. 152pp.
27. Liu, Yingchao, Zheng-Xiang, Li. Laukamp, C., West, G. and Cardoll. S. (2013). *Quantified Spatial Relationships and Key Ore Genesis Controlling Factors and Predictive Mineralisation Mapping, St. Ives Goldfields, Western Australia.* In Ore Geology Reviews, pp,157-166.
28. McKay, B. and Wake, B. (2015). *Intrusion-Related Gold Systems in the New England Fold Belt: The Tooloom Example.* Malachite Resources NL.
29. McQueen, K.G. (2018). *Mining History of the New England Region.* In Geological Report No. 852017/0650. Geological Survey of New South Wales PDF.
30. McQueen, K.G. (2016). *Landscape and Evolution of the Clarence River Catchment Weird Rivers and Wild ideas.* In Fourth Australian Regolith Geoscientists Association Conference. Thredbo. NSW. Institute of Applied Ecology. Univ. of Canberra. Canberra. Australia. pp. 55-59.
31. Meert, J.G., and Torsvik, T.M. (2003). *The Unmaking of a Supercontinent: Rodinia Revisited.* Techno Physics 375(1). pp.261-288.
32. Milan, L.A., Belousova, E.A., Glen, R.A., Chapman, T., Kalmbach, J, Fu, B. and P.M. Ashley (2020). *A New Reconstruction for Permian East Gondwana Based on Zircon Data from Ophiolite of the East Australian Great Serpentinite Belt.. In* Geophysical Research Letters. AGU Journals *at https://agupubs.onlinelibrary.Wiley.com>doi>pdf:*
33. Mustard, R, Neilsen, R and Ruxton, P.A. (1998). *Timbarra Gold Deposits.* In D.A. Berkman and D.A. MacKenzie (Eds.) Geology of Australia and Papua New Guinea Mineral Deposits. The Institute of Mining and Metallurgy. Melbourne. pp.551-560.
34. Mustard, R. (2001). *Granite-hosted, gold mineralization at Timbarra, Northern New South Wales, Australia:* In Mineralium Deposita. V36. pp542-562.
35. Mustard, R. (2004). *Textural, mineralogical and geochemical variation in the zoned Timbarra Tablelands pluton, New South Wales** In Australian Journal of Earth Sciences.
36. Porter Geo Consultancies Pty Ltd. (2004). *Timbarra. Main Commodities: Au.* New South Wales. CRC. 3pp.
37. Roberts, R.H. (1984). *The New England Batholith consists of a multitude of granitoid plutons in the southern New England fold belt.* Thesis. Univ. of New England. Armidale.

38. Robertson, A. D. (1972). T*he Geological Relationships of the New England Batholith and the Economic Mineral Deposits of the Stanthorpe District.* Geological Survey of Queensland. pp.31-38.
39. Rosenbaum, G., PengFei, Li and Rubatto, D. (2012). *The Contorted New England Orogen (Eastern Australia: New evidence from U-Pb geochronology of Early Permian Granitoids.* In Tectonics Vol 31(1). 14pp.
40. Rosenbaum, G. (2012). Oroclines of the Southern New England Orogen, Eastern Australia.
41. Rosenbaum, G. (2018). *The Tasmanides: Phanerozoic Tectonic Evolution of Eastern Australia.* Annual Review of Earth and Planetary Sciences. School of Earth and Environmental Sciences, Univ. of Queensland, Brisbane, Queensland 4072, Australia. Jour. Annu. Rev. Earth Planet. Sci. 2018. 46 pp. 291-325.
42. Stroud, W. J., Barnes, R.G., Browne, R.E., Brownlow J.W., and H.F. Henley. (1999). *Some aspects of the metallogenesis of the southern New England Fold Belt.* In NEO '99 Conference Proceedings. Univ. of New England. Armidale and Geological Survey of NSW, Department of Mineral Resources, Armidale. pp 365-371.
43. Willmott, W. (2017). *Rocks and Landscapes of Stanthorpe and the Granite Belt.* In Geological Society of Australia. Qld Div. 2016.
44. Willmot, W. (2013). Geological map, simplified from illustration on p.455 of Vol. 'Geology of Queensland'.
45. Thomson, J. (1976). Geology of the Drake 1:100000 Sheet. Dept. of Mines. Geological Survey of New South Wales. 185 pp.

Classification of igneous rocks by colour and silica content

Classification of the igneous rocks found in the vicinity of the Tooloom goldfield. These are divided according to colour and by the percentage of free silica in the melt or magma.

For magma (or melt) after cooling	*Felsic types*	*Intermediate types*	*Mafic and Ultra Mafic types*
Colour	Light coloured but may have some dark biotite inclusions. Quartz crystals can be seen in the matrix of the rock. Granite usually has pink orthoclase and white plagioclase crystals in it.	Dark coloured with white phenocrysts (a large crystal of, for example, plagioclase feldspar, set in a finer-grained host rock, which. gives the rock a speckled appearance.	Dark and heavy – May have green glassy phenocrysts of olivine. Associated with rocks of the ocean floors. Ultramafic rocks have less silica than mafic rocks.
% of free SiO_2 in the melt	>65%. This will usually have free quartz in the matrix of the rock.	55-65%	45 to 55% is Mafic <45% is Ultra Mafic
Intrusive example	Granite Tonalite	Diorite	Gabbro (Mafic) Peridotite (Ultra Mafic)
Extrusive or volcanic rock	Rhyolite – the presence of free quartz in the melt makes this magma very sticky and explosive. Dacite	Andesite – This is intermediate between the explosive, sticky lavas and the more fluid dark-coloured mafic basalts.	Basalt -These lavas run freely. They have no free quartz. The free-flowing magmas of Hawaiian Islands are of this type.

Geological terminology

Alluvium versus colluvium: Colluvium is a general name for loose, unconsolidated sediments that have been deposited at the base of hillslopes by either rain wash, sheet wash or slow continuous downslope creep, as opposed to alluvium, which refers to loose sedimentary material that is transported and deposited by glaciers, streams, wind and ocean waves.

Adamellite Granite: A granite rock that is rich in quartz, plagioclase feldspar and potassic feldspar with orthoclase feldspars being < than 10%.

Asthenosphere: The asthenosphere is the mechanically weak and ductile region of the upper mantle of the Earth. It lies below the lithosphere, at a depth between 80 and 200 km below the surface, and extends as deep as 700 km. It is not well defined. The tectonic plates are able to move around on the lithosphere on top of this semi-plastic layer in the Mantle.

Aureole: The thermally metamorphosed (heat affected) contact zone between a pluton or large intrusion and the surrounding country rock. Metamorphism is the changing of a rock due to the effects of heat and/or pressure.

A-Type Granites. These are associated with mafic types of igneous rocks. They probably come from mantle-derived transitional to alkaline mafic to intermediate magmas (From Science Direct and see also Appendices).

Backarc zone: This is an extensional zone on the continental side of a volcanic arc and subduction zone (this author's explanation).

Backarc basin: This is an extensional basin formed on the continental side of a volcanic arc and subduction zone. It collects volcanic detritus (this author's explanation).

Backarc Extension: This occurs when a backarc basin is being thinned under stress by the subducting plate, which also pulls down and thins the upper slab as the subducting slab tries to thrust beneath it. The reader might like to think of this as an example of crustal stretching (This author's simplified explanation).

Batholith: A massive igneous(granitic) intrusion of unknown depth in the crust.

Bimodal Magmatism: Bimodal volcanism is *the eruption of both mafic and felsic lava from a single volcanic centre with little or no lava of intermediate composition.* These are associated with rifting (Academic Accelerator Encyclopedia).

Breccia pipe: A depositional, hydrothermal structure sometimes called a chimney that consists of a mass of fragments of a mineral or of the local bedrock, which has subsequently then been cemented together. It often has an irregular shape and is thought to have been formed via the fracturing of the bedrock during the passage of high-pressure, hydrothermal fluids through the rocks in that area. These hot fluids are usually generated by the presence of an underlying igneous intrusion.

Clast: This is simply a typical rock fragment that has been taken from any sedimentary rock layer (This author).

Disseminated gold: This describes an ore where small particles of valuable minerals have been spread quite uniformly throughout the host rock. (Futura-Sciences.US).

Devonian-Carboniferous: These periods of the Palaeozoic are recognised in this study as a continuing time zone in the geological history of the southern New England Orogeny in north-eastern New South Wales.

Extrusive: Igneous rocks that are erupted and cool on or very close to, the surface.

Epithermal gold: Low sulphide epithermal gold deposits are derived from reduced, near neutral pH, dilute fluids, which are developed by the presence of magmatic components within deep circulating groundwaters; this is then characterised by the sulphur component being reduced to H_2S gas.

Forearc basin: This is a sedimentary basin in a subduction zone between an oceanic trench and its associated volcanic arc.

Fractionation: In the slow cooling of a magma, heavier minerals form first and these then drop down out of the chemical reaction in the melt. This then becomes more silica rich as fractionation proceeds.

Fractionated Granites: As magma is intruded and then starts to cool, the heavy mafic minerals begin to crystallise first. Eventually, these sink to the bottom of the magma chamber, thus leaving behind a magma or melt that becomes increasingly depleted of these dark minerals. Over time, the magma thus becomes more felsic in character. Leucogranites are an end-result.

Gondwanaland: A large Palaeozoic supercontinent in the southern hemisphere. Australia split from Gondwanaland due to rifting at approximately 99 Ma. (or Million years ago)

Granitoid: This is any coarse-grained granitic intrusion of undefined size.

Hydrothermal gold: As magmas cool and crystallise, hot water-rich fluids can be released. These can be rich in various minerals such as sulphur, sodium, copper, tin, silver, stibnite and gold. Hydrothermal fluids also dissolve other elements as they flow through the country rocks and then cool and deposit this gold etc in hydrothermal deposits. (Libre Texts Geosciences).

Greisen deposit: These form in granitoid rocks in which >90% of the feldspar is replaced by quartz, mica, topaz, cassiterite and by other minerals. A greisen is sometimes capped by pegmatites; these can form in the roof zone of some granitic plutons.

Intrusive igneous rocks: These cool and solidify below the surface of the earth,

Leucogranite: These are light-coloured granites that have been highly fractionated to the stage where there are no dark Mafic minerals left in them.

~ **200 Ma**: means the equivalence of 200 million years ago.

Mesozoic Triassic: The Triassic is the first period in the Mesozoic era.

Mesothermal deposits: These deposits are formed by hot water moving through the rocks as the surrounding rocks were uplifted from deep (10 km plus) in the Earth's crust. The metals in the deposits were extracted from the surrounding rocks by the dissolution of trace amounts of minerals from a large volume of rocks. (Environ. Geology. Univ. Otago. NZ).

Monzogranite: These are granites that are fractionated down to the final fractionated stage of a cooling magma or melt; they are usually felsic.

Neoproterozoic Era: This is the unit of geologic time from 1 billion to 538.8 million years ago.

Obduction: The sideways and downward movement of the edge of a crustal plate into the mantle beneath another plate. (Oxford Languages Dictionary).

Orogeny and Orogen: A mountain building zone and period.

Oroclines: An orocline is a thrust belt or orogen that is curved in map-view due to it having been bent or buckled about a vertical axis of rotation (GeoScienceWorld).

Palaeozoic: This is a major component of earth's history or Era. It ran from approximately 538,8 to 251 million years ago. This term stands for 'Ancient Life'.

Silurian Palaeozoic: The Silurian was a period in the Middle Palaeozoic era.

Peel Manning Fault System : This is a major Australian fault system that is 350 kms long. It separates the Silurian sediments from the Carboniferous sediments of the Tamworth Belt in the west from the Silurian to Carboniferous wedge sediments of the accretionary Tablelands Complex to the east.

Plate: The earth's outer shell was cracked in the very early, pre-Palaeozoic times into a number of large pieces or plates that are able to move more freely around the surface of this planet by sliding over a less viscos layer in the middle mantle zone called the asthenosphere. Each plate can vary in size and can consist of continental crust (not always) and of oceanic material below the crust, which is a part of the upper mantle down to the sliding asthenosphere layer.

Pluton: This is any igneous intrusion such as a batholith, but this could also be a dyke - a narrow vertical intrusion cutting vertically across the sedimentary layers or as a sill, which is a lateral intrusion between two sedimentary layers.

Subduction: This is a process where two plates meet and one plate can be subducted or forced down into the upper mantle under another in a thrust/shear fault zone. Here, the subducted plate can subsequently then melt into the mantle zone. Sometimes, two plates can just converge and, with subsequent compression, there is folding and uplift of the continental sediments that are trapped between them, thus giving rise to high mountain zones like the Himalayas in Northern India.

Subvolcanic rock: This also known as a hyperbyssal rock, which is an intrusive igneous rock that is emplaced at depths less than 2 km within the crust – an example is diorite. This can have a porphyry texture.

Sericite alteration: This is a process of mineralisation caused by a hydrothermal fluid invading a permeable country rock.

Skarn: This is a zone of alteration in the metamorphic contact zone (or aureole) around a big intrusion when carbonate sedimentary rocks are invaded by large amounts of aluminium, silica and iron. These form from the interactions of hot hydrothermal fluids.

Stockworks: These are a network of small thin veins of gold-bearing quartz and can comprise a complex system of structurally controlled or randomly oriented veins. The veins in the stockworks are thinner than are gold lodes.

Rifting: This is the splitting apart of a single tectonic plate into two or more tectonic plates separated by divergent plate boundaries (By ScienceDirect). This process is associated with bimodal volcanism (by this author).

Slab breakoff: The subducting plate (usually oceanic) will be heavier than the crustal plate on top and this often causes the subducting plate to break off and to descend at a faster rate into the mantle than its crustal companion (by this author).

Slab Rollback: This refers to the process that involves an older oceanic crust, which is colder and more dense than other slabs, subducting at a steeper angle. As the older slab collapses into the asthenosphere, it can "roll back" through the mantle (By eHow).

Tectonic divisor: See the Peel Manning Fault System in NSW.

Terrane: When an existing continent such as Rodinia broke apart in the Iapetus Ocean in the Pre-Palaeozoic Era, it was eventually broken up into individual chunks or terranes as the subduction of the Rodinian plate proceeded. The terranes that resulted may then have travelled long distances on the remaining oceanic areas of their previous slabs. They are distinguished by having sharp, bounding fault lines, which mark a section of the continental crust that broke apart and which are usually the site for lateral movement of the blocks along strike faults. They are usually individually different from the neighbouring terranes in their mineral occurrences and in their geological history.

Tonalites: These are felsic intrusive rocks, which are found in a granitoid area with < 10% of orthoclase feldspar and > 20% silica or quartz. The extrusive type of this magma is usually a dacite.

Volcanoclastic rock: This is igneous rock that has been erupted into the air. Another name for this would be a pyroclastic rock. This lava is often intermixed with small clasts of country rock sediments.

Wedge sediments: An accretionary wedge is the build-up of sediment scrapped from an oceanic plate by the overriding plate during the process of subduction. As the accretionary wedge grows, it is the underside that collects new sediment from the subducting oceanic plate (Study.com).

A Toast to the Diggers

The Roaring Days

by Henry Lawson

The night too quickly passes
And we are growing old,
So let us lift our glasses
And toast the Days of Gold;
When finds of wondrous treasure
Set all the South ablaze,
And you and I were faithful mates
All through those roaring days!

More fitting words could not be written, than those of Lawson, to evoke memories of those *Roaring Days.* Consequently, we regularly use this toast around the campfire, when out on the diggings.

Garry Gatfield

Published by
Grosvenor Creation

Email: goldpan@outlook.com

About the Author

This author retired in 2006 after 37 years in Telecommunications. He was a Principal Telecommunications Technical Officer and Shift Leader in a major fault repair centre. His most notable customer was President Bill Clinton, whilst he was on holidays in North Qld. In 1982, he was one of the four Technical Officers who manned the Commonwealth Games Fault Centre at Woolloongabba.

As a NBLC member, Garry Gatfield has served as President of North Brisbane Lapidary Club Inc for four terms and is currently the Field Trips Officer and is a Faceting Instructor. He is a member of the Australian Facetor's Guild - a club with over 700 members; he regularly lectures on the subjects of gold and diamonds in Australia.

Garry's hobbies include genealogy, gold, mineral and gem fossicking, faceting, caravanning and camping, woodwork, and writing.

This author has previously written articles for Gold, Gem and Treasure Magazine, as well as, for Facet Talk - the bi-monthly magazine for the Australian Facetor's Guild. Garry has been interviewed on radio a number of times on the subject of gold nuggets.

The author panning a half ounce nugget from a Clarence River goldfield

Source: Garry Gatfield, 2024

www.ingramcontent.com/pod-product-compliance
Ingram Content Group UK Ltd.
Pitfield, Milton Keynes, MK11 3LW, UK
UKHW062009290726
14090UKWH00022B/1467

9 780648 318415